To Katie
with fondest good wishes

Moira Anderson

Christmas 1981.

MOIRA ANDERSON'S SCOTLAND

MOIRA ANDERSON'S SCOTLAND

Moira Anderson
with Netta Martin

LUTTERWORTH PRESS
Guildford & London

FOR MY MOTHER AND FATHER

Lutterworth Press
Luke House, Farnham Road, Guildford, GU1 4XD

Designed and produced for Lutterworth Press by
Bellew & Higton Publishers Ltd, 19-21 Conway Street
London W1P 6JD

ISBN 0-7188-2518-7

Set in 11pt ACM Souvenir Light
Colour separations by Fotographics Ltd.
Printed in Scotland by Morrison & Gibb Ltd.

ACKNOWLEDGEMENTS

Moira Anderson and Netta Martin would like to thank the Dumfries and Galloway Tourist Association, the Mid-Argyll, Kintyre and Islay Tourist Organization, the Kyle and Carrick District Council, the Perth Tourist Association, the Isle of Skye Tourist Organization, the Sutherland Tourist Organization and the Tourist Division of the Tayside Regional Council for reading and commenting on the manuscript, and, in particular, Mr John Hutchinson, Publications Editor of the Scottish Tourist Board, for his invaluable help and suggestions when the book was in proof.

The authors and publishers are grateful to the following for permission to reproduce photographs:
Dmitri Kasterine, pages 1, 2, 10-11, 12, 14-15, 15 *right*, 24-5, 26, 30, 33, 34, 35, 36-7, 40-1, 46, 54, 57, 64, 78, 95 *right*, 96, 98-9, 104 *left*, 114, 122, 128 *left*, 152, 154-5, 156 and 157.
Dave Paterson, pages 6-7, 8, 11 *right*, 13, 18, 47, 70-1, 74-5, 76, 79, 80-1, 83, 100-1, 106, 109, 124-5, 131, 132-3, 134-5, 136-7, 140-1, 143, 147 and 148-9.
British Tourist Authority, pages 16-17, 20-1, 28-9, 32, 112-13, 126 and 130.
J. Allan Cash, pages 22-3, 27, 38, 42, 44-5, 48, 49, 51, 128-9 and 138.
Sonia Halliday, pages 72, 90, 97, 102, 117, 118 and 120-1.
Margaret Hunter, page 145.
Jorge Lewinski, pages 56, 58-9, 62-3 and 93.
Mike McQueen, pages 69, 84-5, 86-7, 110-11 and 150-1.

Scottish Tourist Board, pages 104-5 and 116.
David Stephen, page 154 *left*.
David Webster, pages 52-3, 60-1, 88-9 and 94-5.

The photographs that open each chapter are as follows: pages 6-7, Loch Dunvegan, Skye (Dave Paterson); pages 16-17, Port Bannatyne, Isle of Bute (British Tourist Authority); pages 28-9, Loch Lomond, on the west coast between Tarbet and Ardlui (British Tourist Authority); pages 40-1, Grampians (Dmitri Kasterine); pages 52-3, Arran Hills, Ayrshire coast (David Webster); pages 62-3, Glencoe (Jorge Lewinski); pages 74-5, Castlebay, Barra (Dave Paterson); pages 88-9, winter scene, near Schiehallion, Aberfeldy (David Webster); pages 100-1, 'Scott's View', across the Tweed towards the Eildon Hills (Dave Paterson); pages 112-13, Kirkcudbright (British Tourist Authority); pages 124-5, Brora (Dave Paterson); pages 136-7, Edinburgh in the mist (Dave Paterson); pages 150-1, Glencoe, evening (Mike McQueen).

Thanks are also due to the following publishers for permission to quote lines from the following songs: Sir Hugh S. Roberton's Trust and Roberton Publications for 'Westering Home' and 'Marie's Wedding'; Bosworth & Co. Ltd. for 'Bonnie Gallowa''; J.B. Cramer & Co. Ltd. for 'The Skye Boat Song'; Boosey & Hawkes Music Publishers Ltd. for 'My Ain Folk', words by Wilfrid Mills. 'Eriskay Love Lilt' reprinted from *Songs of the Hebrides* by permission of the Trustees of the Estate of Marjory Kennedy-Fraser and Boosey & Hawkes Music Publishers Ltd.

CONTENTS

THE SKYE BOAT SONG

Speed bonnie boat like a bird on the wing,
'Onward,' the sailors cry,
Carry the lad that's born to be King
Over the sea to Skye.

When the Vikings first saw the cloud-capped Cuillins of Skye, they called the place the 'Misty Isle'. For many people, that name still conjures up the perfect image of Skye: a mysterious Scottish island shrouded in mists, steeped in legend and dominated by a castle, the ancestral home of the clan MacLeod.

When I was a child, my imagination was fired by the stories of Bonnie Prince Charlie, the Young Pretender who tried to rally the Scottish clans to drive out the English and restore the Stuarts to the British throne. Bonnie Prince Charlie's famous association with Skye was a result of his defeat at Culloden in 1746, after which he crossed sea and mountain to escape from the Hanoverians. It was while he was hiding in Uist that Flora Macdonald helped him escape 'over the sea to Skye'.

For me, it was the man himself that mattered, not what he stood for politically. I saw him as a handsome fugitive being hunted by the wicked invaders. He was the hero who inspired such loyalty that even the poorest Scot would not have dreamt of betraying him for the £30,000 ransom set on his head.

As I grew up, I began to have second thoughts about Bonnie Prince Charlie — the grand laddie whose picture appears on so many tins of Scottish shortbread. He stands there proudly at the prow of a rowing boat, immaculately dressed, with never a hair of his wig out of place. And there is that poor woman, Flora Macdonald, rowing her heart out to get him over the sea to Skye. In pictures, Flora looks fragile enough to be felled by a butterfly's wing: if she really *did* row the Prince over the sea to Skye, she must have been well fortified by Drambuie and porridge; moreover, the incident does not show the Prince in a very chivalrous light.

Then I visited Skye with a teaching colleague, Isabel Sillars, and the romance of the legend bewitched me all over again. Skye is fifty miles long and, next to Lewis and Harris, the largest island in the Hebrides. It is rather like a giant starfish, with fingers of land pointing out in all directions — as a result of which no part is more than five miles from the sea.

Even the peninsulas have haunting names: Trotternish, Vaternish, Duirinish, Minguish, Strathaird and Sleat. If you approach Skye from the Outer Hebridean islands of Harris or Uist, you arrive in the north of Skye at Uig in Trotternish, but most visitors land on the east coast of the island on ferries from Mallaig and Kyle of Lochalsh on the Scottish mainland.

It was from Kyle of Lochalsh that I sailed over the sea on my first trip to Skye. This was the time in my life when I had just begun teaching music in Ayrshire and my professional singing career was still ahead of me.

My only concern that bright summer morning was money: the lack of it. Teachers in these days were not particularly well paid and Isabel and I were both in the same financial boat. However, after discussing the holiday and doing some frantic calculations, we had decided we could manage a fortnight in Skye if we went by car (petrol was relatively cheap) and stayed at cottages offering bed and breakfast at reasonable terms. The views were magnificent as we drove up the west coast of Scotland and we arrived at Kyle of Lochalsh in the highest of spirits.

The trip from Kyle of Lochalsh to Kyleakin takes a mere five minutes, since the Straits of Kyleakin are just half a mile wide. They take their name from Hakon, a king of Norway who sailed through them on his way to the battle of Largs in 1263. Kyleakin itself is a quaint little village, but we decided to make our way south along the Sound of Sleat. Sleat has been called the garden of Skye and the fields and hedgerows were brimming over with wild flowers. Even the woods seemed soft and green.

On the Isle of Skye near Glendale - a brilliant array of summer flowers.

We passed through the cluster of crofts at Isleornsay and went to Knock, where we stopped at the ruins of Camus Castle. Camus used to belong to the MacLeods until the Macdonalds took it away from them. It was the same story at Ord on the west coast of Sleat: the MacLeods lost possession to the Macdonalds.

We were lucky at Ord, which gave us our first full view of the Cuillins – and on a day when the sun was shining. Yet not even the gentle gold of sunlight can soften the impact of the razor-sharp Cuillins, a score of strangely shaped peaks and rock spires soaring up against the skyline. Surely the Cuillins must be the most impressive mountain range in Britain, for nowhere else do mountains dominate such a large tract of land. Wherever we went in Skye, we found ourselves looking up at them or back at them.

What fascinated me was the way light and shade kept changing their aspect. At Ord, when

the Cuillins were bathed in sunlight, they were gentle strangers' beckoning to us invitingly, but later when we were exploring the Strathaird peninsula which divides Loch Slapin from Loch Scavaig, dark clouds made the scarred peaks black and menacing like an army of angry giants.

It was to Elgol in Strathaird that Bonnie Prince Charlie finally came during his stay in Skye, and it was here that I realized I had got the Flora Macdonald story all wrong.

Flora had been asked by Lady Margaret Macdonald, wife of the clan chief, to bring the Young Pretender back to Skye. In Uist, when Flora was arrested by the Hanoverian troops, she not only fooled them into thinking that Bonnie Prince Charlie was her serving maid, Betty Burke, but she managed to persuade the commander to give them a pass to return to Skye.

But it was not fragile Flora who rowed Bonnie Prince Charlie over the sea to Skye. It was five strong men of Uist who acted as her crew. When they landed at Uig in Trotternish on the northeast of Skye, everything went wrong. The Prince should have gone to Lady Macdonald at Monkstadt House, but government troops were there before him.

Bonnie Prince Charlie had to cross the island to Portree and then hide out on the neighbouring island of Raasay before making his way south to Elgol in the Strathaird peninsula. At Elgol, the clan Mackinnon gave him a banquet in a cave and then rowed him in a boat over to the mainland, from where he escaped to the Continent.

Left The soaring presence of the Cuillins - visible almost everywhere on Skye. *Below* Elgol, where Bonnie Prince Charlie embarked for the mainland.

Flora Macdonald was arrested and imprisoned, but at least there is a happy ending to her story. After two years she was released and later she married her kinsman Allan Macdonald of Kingsburgh. She had seven children and a happy life, which is more than can be said for Bonnie Prince Charlie. On the big Celtic cross which is Flora Macdonald's tombstone is an inscription by Dr Johnson: 'A name that will be mentioned in history, and if courage and fidelity be virtues, mentioned with honour.'

Chatting with a peat-cutter, Mr Stoddart, by his newly-dug trench. He is leaning on a peat-iron.

We were anxious to see all the places connected with Flora Macdonald and the Prince: Elgol in the south, Uig in the north and, to the east, Portree. And of course we wanted to see Dunvegan Castle and villages such as Broadford, one of the biggest crofting townships on the island. So we toured during the day and at about five o'clock we would begin our hunt for lodgings.

Since we had arrived on the island we had been lucky with finding places to stay. When I think of Skye today I have memories of trim white cottages, cosy sitting-rooms and enormous breakfasts: all this and a bed for just over £1.

Yet even in these days, although Skye folk were friendly, they had their own method of I.V.A. – instant visual assessment. We had heard that if the crofters did not like the look of you, they would hum and haw and tell you blandly that the 'Vacancies' notice in the window was a wee thing out of date and they were full up.

We must have looked as innocent and trusting as we were in those days, because I do not recall ever being turned away. On one occasion at the end of a long, hot day we arrived at one white-washed croft to discover a 'No Vacancies' sign on its door. Disaster: there was not another house in sight. We were exhausted, and so we knocked at the door and explained our predicament to the owner. She listened to us sympathetically, subjected us to a few searching enquiries and at the end of them said: 'Och, well now, I just might find a wee bittie room for you somewhere.' To our astonishment, she then proceeded to offer us a choice of three empty bedrooms! The Skye folk are a law unto themselves.

My most embarrassing moment in Skye happened when we lodged with a minister and his wife for bed and breakfast. They were so kind to us that we stayed with them for several days. While we were there, we visited the nearby peat bogs where someone told us that there is nothing on earth to equal the warm, scented smell of a peat fire burning in your grate on a cold winter's evening. On the last morning of our stay with the minister, we stopped the car at the side of a road and saw an enormous pile of freshly-cut peat clods. We looked at them longingly, visualizing them burning fragrantly in our fireplaces at home and the next minute we were secreting a few in the boot. Surely, we thought, no one would notice that half a dozen were missing...

We bade farewell to the minister and his wife after lunch and he graciously carried our suitcases out to the car. We opened the boot, completely forgetting what we had packed inside, and there lay the stolen clods of peat. It is to the minister's credit that his expression did not change and he did not utter one word of reproof. There was no need. Our faces flamed like a Skye sunset as we drove towards Portree.

Portree, the capital of the island, was given its name after King James V visited it in 1540. Thereafter it was called the Port of the King, which later became abbreviated (from the Gaelic) to Portree. Flora Macdonald supposedly bade farewell to Bonnie Prince Charlie in what is now a room in a Portree hotel. He is reported to have lent dignity to the occasion by giving her a miniature of himself and expressing the hope that one day he would be able to welcome her to the Court of St James. Everyone spoke of his courage and courtesy.

At this stage of our holiday, I was beginning to revise my earlier scepticism about the Young Pretender and Flora Macdonald. Whatever the rights or wrongs of their cause, they were both immensely brave, and somehow, the minute you step on Skye, you are willing to believe the best about them.

A lock of the Prince's hair is on display at the last place we visited, Dunvegan Castle.

Dunvegan, the ancestral home of the clan MacLeod, is probably the most famous place in Skye. It lies on Skye's west coast between the two peninsulas of Vaternish and Duirinish, and it impressed me as being every bit as formidable as its clan chief at that time, Dame Flora MacLeod of MacLeod. Built on the shore of Loch Dunvegan, it has a big, square tower which looms over the battlements and walls of up to ten feet thick.

The Skye dynasty of MacLeods was founded through Leod, Olav the Black's son, who acquired Dunvegan Castle when he married the daughter of its owner. Their son, Tormad MacLeod, was the first chieftain, but Dame Flora, who died in 1976 at the age of 98, was certainly the best known. She rallied MacLeods from all over the world to clan gatherings at Dunvegan and travelled the world fostering interest in her clan.

Although the clan system operated in Scotland for nearly five hundred years, its origins are

At Portree, Skye's capital. Loading fresh-caught giant prawns, a speciality of this area.

vague. Some clans formed naturally when groups of Highlanders with a common name and ancestry decided to band together for their own protection. Other clans came into being when they conquered neighbouring tribes or married into them. Sometimes the conferment of a royal favour was responsible for a clan's formation.

By the time the Hebrides were given back to Scotland by the Norsemen, in the thirteenth century, the clans were feuding and fighting with each other and the history of Skye, like that of the rest of the Hebrides, is one of bloody battles between the MacLeods, the Macdonalds and the Mackinnons.

The castle's treasures are unique to Skye and to the MacLeods. On display, apart from the yellow lock of Bonnie Prince Charlie's hair cut off by Flora Macdonald, is the sword and drinking horn of Rory Mor, the twelfth chief. The cup, chased with silver, holds five gills of claret, which each new chief must down in a draught at his in-auguration. The present one, John MacLeod of MacLeod (grandson of Dame Flora), drank it in 1 minute 57 seconds.

The most fascinating relic in the castle was, for me, the famous Fairy Flag. The stories about it are legion. One of them claims that when a Mac-Leod chief fell in love with a fairy and had to part from her, she covered their child with the Fairy Flag and endowed it with magical properties. It would bring herring into the loch, grant children to the heir, or gain victory for the MacLeods on a battlefield. With the wish came a warning: the flag could be waved only to save the clan or the chief from death or destruction, and only on three occasions.

Left A Skye landscape, dotted with crofts. *Below* Dunvegan Castle, ancestral home of the MacLeods, which I visited one wet summer's day.

Some say it has been waved three times already, but others claim that the Fairy Flag has been used only twice. The only point on which everyone seems to agree is that it was definitely waved in 1597 at Trumpan when the Macdonalds set fire to a church in which the MacLeods worshipped, and by that act killed all but one of them − the exception being a young woman who escaped to wave the Fairy Flag, whereupon the MacLeods from Dunvegan swooped down and killed all the Macdonalds.

I would love to have lived in those stirring times when the MacLeods and Macdonalds were fighting for possession of the island of Skye, but I certainly would not have gone near Dunvegan Castle to visit the MacLeods. You see, my married name is Macdonald!

MULL OF KINTYRE

Mull of Kintyre
Oh mist rolling in from the sea...

My first encounter with the Beatles was after I had just completed a recording session with George Martin at the Abbey Road studios in London. As we were leaving, George said, 'You must come and meet some boys from Liverpool who are going to make quite a name for themselves one day.' The boys were setting up for their session and there seemed nothing remarkable about them − until they started to play. The sound was quite overwhelming and I was rocked back on my heels by the terrific enthusiasm of their performance.

Just how fantastically successful the Beatles became is now part of history. They introduced an entirely new sound and their records sold in millions throughout the world. For years they dominated the pop scene until they eventually decided to go their separate ways.

Paul McCartney, in particular, maintained a continuous involvement with performing and song-writing, but he decided after a time that he needed a retreat from the London scene. For this reason he bought a remote farmhouse in Kintyre, a forty-mile peninsula of land which hangs like a long, oblong leaf from Tarbert in Argyll, on the south-west coast of Scotland. From their isolated house near Campbeltown, the McCartneys sent their children to the local school and blended in with the country background. They managed to keep a certain amount of privacy until Paul decided to write a song about the place he had grown to love, the Mull of Kintyre.

The song was a million beats away from the Beatles' first record but it was an instant and sensational success. The words and music captured ideally the beauty and loneliness of these shores and appealed strongly to the longing in all of us to 'get away from it all'.

Since the song was published, thousands of people have come to Scotland looking for the Mull of Kintyre. People are apt to talk of the whole of Kintyre as the Mull, but in fact the Mull lies at the extreme south-west tip of the Kintyre peninsula and is only a small part of it.

Nor is it the easiest place to find. Southend, the nearest point of habitation, is a little holiday village with sandy beaches, an hotel and a golf course. Nearby are the remains of a castle, a ruined chapel, the traces of a Druid altar, and a flat stone on which you can see two footprints. Some say these are the footprints of Columba, made when he came over from Ireland to convert the Scots to Christianity; others say they are marks made by pre-Christian chiefs who took their vows here. Whatever they may be, there is an atmosphere about the Druid altar, the castle and the ruined chapel which make it an eerie place.

Opposite Southend are the tiny islands of Sanda and Sheep, but if you want to reach the Mull of Kintyre itself you have to go westwards. Then you climb down a steep track to the lighthouse, from which you have a magnificent view of the Mull and of the coast of Ireland, only thirteen miles distant. Visible off the Irish coast is Rathlin Island, one of Robert the Bruce's hiding-places. Even people who know nothing about Scottish history know the tale of Robert the Bruce, who, in deep despair one day, sat in a cave watching a spider and gained new hope and courage from its tireless determination. But where was this cave? There are various places round Scotland which claim the honour, but Rathlin Island is probably the strongest contender.

To explore the peninsula of Kintyre, you have to travel north from Southend to Campbeltown on the east coast. Before you reach Campbeltown, you will see the cave of St Kiaran, another missionary who came to convert the Scots. There is no doubt that a great number of well-meaning religious men had the same mission. It cannot have been an easy job, judging from the lawless ways of our wild ancestors.

In later years, too, men of God kept trying to point Scots towards religion. Davaar Island

Sunset on the south of the Kintyre peninsula.

boasts another cave, in which one Archibald MacKinnon painted the Crucifixion scene in the nineteenth century. Its most intriguing feature is the way it is lit: the cave is dark until sunlight streams through a natural cavity in the rock and illuminates the picture.

Davaar Island, with its unusual cave, is at the mouth of Campbeltown Loch and here I must pay tribute to Andy Stewart, a friend and fellow artist. Andy, who has travelled all over the world singing Scottish songs, is very much aware of the hard-drinking image that Scots present to the world and some imp of mischief made Andy write a song about it, 'Campbeltown Loch':

Campbeltown loch, I wish you were whisky,
Campbeltown loch, och aye!
Campbeltown loch, I wish you were whisky —
I would drink you dry.

The shape of Campbeltown Loch, with Davaar Island at its mouth, gives Campbeltown sheltered anchorage and it has long been the headquarters of a busy fishing fleet. There are merchants' warehouses and chandlers' shops round the picturesque quay.

My most vivid memory of Campbeltown is the day I flew there from Glasgow for the wedding of a nursing sister, a colleague of my husband's. The idea was to stay for the wedding and then fly back to Glasgow the same day. We should have known that after a wedding in a place like Campbeltown we had no hope getting back that night. After the ceremony photographs were taken and there was a sumptuous dinner which seemed to go on for hours, speeches full of Highland humour which made us rock with laughter, and then, of course, there was the dancing...

Anyone who has ever watched Scottish country dancing appreciates that what you need are strong legs, strong arms and a strong voice to keep shouting above the din. You get some idea of the vigorous mood of such celebration in a favourite song of mine, 'Marie's Wedding'.

Step we gaily as we go,
Heel for heel and toe for toe,
Arm in arm and row on row,
All for Marie's wedding.

Over hillways up and down,
Myrtle green and bracken brown,
Past the shieling through the town,
All for sake of Marie.

Campbeltown, Strathclyde: the Old Quay, from which herring, white fish and lobsters are caught.

During the dancing, the locals kept telling me about the places I should visit, and mentioned that Kintyre, with its backbone of bracken-clad hills, has good roads running along the east and west shores.

'Mind, you have to be careful driving up the east,' an old worthy cautioned me. 'It's a terrible road for bends and hills. But you get some lovely

views of the Kilbrannan Sound. That's the one that separates Kintyre from Arran and in places it's only three miles wide.'

'And do you go to Arran often?' I asked politely.

'Never been there in my life,' he replied, obviously amazed at the suggestion that he should ever have forsaken his beloved Kintyre.

He was so obviously wanting to tell me about the area that I did not like to reveal that I had actually travelled up the east coast of Kintyre; indeed, I had found the drive most exciting with its sudden swoops down to sea-level and up again. We have friends who used to go to Carradale for their holidays every year and it is probably the most popular holiday resort in the whole of Kintyre. The houses and hotels are set amidst lush greenery, there are facilities for fishing, boating and sailing, and there is a beautiful beach called Silver Sands. Best of all, there are no crowds.

The road north from Carradale leads to Claonaig, where a car ferry will transport you to

the neighbouring island of Arran in twenty minutes.

The next day, Stuart and I reluctantly decided we had to leave the wedding festivities. We set off by car from Campbeltown on the east coast for Machrihanish on the west. The route is through the laggan or hollow of Kintyre and the land is fertile and flat. In former years there used to be a unique little railway which ran across the laggan and this formed part of a delightful day-excursion from Arran, terminating at Machrihanish. But Machrihanish is easy enough to reach by car. Moreover, it is a pleasant place to linger because it is not the kind of Scots village you expect to see on a lonely peninsula. It has a row of magnificent stone houses which used to belong to the merchant princes of Glasgow, who lived there in some style. Only a road separates them from a sandy shore and the Atlantic, and behind the houses is one of Scotland's finest golf courses. It was laid out in 1876 and the scenery (not to mention the turf) is so fine that the course draws many holiday-makers not just from Scotland but from much further afield too.

From Machrihanish airport, you can fly to Glasgow in forty minutes, but although the journey by road takes four hours, it is much more rewarding.

If the Kintyre peninsula is like a long oblong leaf, Tarbert is the twig at the top. Only a narrow line of land links Kintyre with the region of Knapdale to the north and prevents it from being an island. The name Tarbert means an isthmus of land; this isthmus irritated one of the kings of Norway, who rejoiced in the name of Magnus Barefoot. Magnus had been given the right of sovereignty over any land he could circumnavigate, but he could not circumnavigate Kintyre because of that annoying stretch of land at its head. However, since Magnus coveted Kintyre, he decided he was not going to be deterred by a mere three-mile isthmus, so he dragged his ships across it and then claimed sovereignty. As far as he was concerned, Kintyre *was* an island. Amazingly, this subterfuge worked and Kintyre remained a Norwegian possession until 1263. Even today, once you head south from Tarbert you begin to feel cut off from 'the mainland'.

Tarbert, a busy fishing port and anchorage, lies at the head of an inlet of Loch Fyne, which is forty-two miles in length and the longest sea loch

Tarbert, between Loch Fyne and West Loch Tarbert.

in Scotland. Across the narrow isthmus is West Loch Tarbert which opens on to the Atlantic and from which the Islay ferries ply.

From Tarbert the road to Glasgow runs up the shores of Loch Fyne through Ardrishaig, the southern terminal of the Crinan Canal, and Lochgilphead, which grew from a small fishing community to become the administrative centre of Argyll. Then comes Crarae, where I always try to stop to admire the rhododendrons or azaleas and ornamental shrubs in the forest and lodge gardens. The gardens, which are open to the public, were created by the present laird's father, Sir George Campbell of Succoth, and I love the way he has put plants, flowers and trees round waterfalls and rustic bridges. It gives the effect of a glorious wild garden in which all the colours harmonize. I am particularly fond of wild gardens and we have tried to create one, on a small scale, in the grounds of our own home in Renfrewshire.

Beyond Crarae, the road turns inland to Auchindrain. This once deserted Highland village has been renovated and restored; it has a byre and different types of dwellings including cottar houses, and, inside them, period furnishings right down to kitchenware and patchwork quilts. The Scottish Life Museum Trust started this project, not knowing whether there would be any great interest in it. Now, so many people travel from far and wide to see it that the Trust has set up centres there where you can see the old crafts being practised and hear how farmers lived and worked in bygone times.

A few miles down the road and you are on the lochside again at Inveraray, my favourite spot on Loch Fyne. I visited it as a child and later with a BBC television unit which was making a film about Burns. The BBC wanted to use Inveraray Castle's kitchens because it has such a marvellous collection of eighteenth-century copper utensils. The present Duke's father was there and one of his aims was to make sure we pronounced Inveraray the proper way: 'Inver-erra.'

In fact, whether you have personal connections with Inveraray or not, it will always be one of the highlights of any tour of Scotland because so much about the town and castle is both superb and unique.

Inveraray town, for example, was custom-built in the eighteenth century by the 3rd Duke of Argyll, chief of the clan Campbell. When he decided to rebuild Inveraray Castle, he made up his mind to remove the clutter of buildings, the old Inveraray village, from beneath the castle windows. He chose the site for his new town well. At the mouth of the river Aray, half a mile from the castle, is a headland on the loch surrounded by green countryside: that is where the Duke commanded his workforce to build. Since his architects for town and castle included men of genius like William Adam, followed by his son John, Roger Morris and Robert Mylne, the castle and the cluster of whitewashed buildings are in delightful harmony with the hills, woodland and water.

Indeed, the town is quite elegant with its Georgian houses and Episcopalian church, whose peal of ten bells commemorates the Campbells who fell in the First World War.

The parish church is *not* elegant, but I have had a soft spot for it ever since I was told that it

once had a dividing wall down its middle so that services in English and Gaelic could be conducted simultaneously. Now Gaelic may be a very melodious language, but the thought of those services in both tongues is rather disconcerting. I cannot help wondering whether each choir tried to sing louder and so outdo the other.

It was singing, of course, which took me to Inveraray Castle. Concerts in a town hall are one thing, but to sing in a Campbell stronghold was positively daunting. After all, here I was, a Macdonald by marriage, in the seat of Campbell's kingdom! Happily the present clan chief, Iain, Duke of Argyll, shares my sense of humour and when we first met we had a good laugh about the fact that a Macdonald and a Campbell could get on so well together.

I had the chance to get to know him better when Stuart and I spent a weekend in the castle as his guests.

The castle is picturesquely situated amidst rolling parkland and trees, and the drive up to the front entrance is extremely impressive.

After a warm welcome by our hosts, the Duke's butler escorted us to our room, and to my horror he began to unpack our bags. I say 'to my horror' because there had been some last-minute crisis and I had hurriedly thrown (and I do mean thrown) our clothes into the suitcases, quite haphazardly. Now the Duke's man was unpacking them, and discovering that whatever else Moira Anderson was, she was not a careful packer. Being a true gentleman, however, he did not allow his face to betray his feelings.

That night we slept well in a magnificent four-poster bed, but were awakened by a peculiar wailing sound. Now my husband has complained in the past about my sleeping habits. Sometimes I dig my elbow into him, and on this occasion I opened my eyes in alarm in case this time I

Helping to hustle some sheep on Kintyre.

really had done him a serious injury. But I soon realized that the sound was coming from outside our window. It was a kilted piper striding up and down, playing his bagpipes. He was our alarm clock to summon us to breakfast.

Over breakfast the Duke talked to us about his family and the castle before taking us on a personally conducted tour of the castle and grounds, an inheritance that was nearly lost to him and to

With the Duke of Argyll at Inveraray.

the nation. In 1975 the Duke had to endure the worst disaster in his family's history when fire broke out in the castle, destroying the roof and causing the loss of many valuable paintings and much fine furniture. Inveraray Castle ablaze must have been a traumatic sight for the Duke and Duchess. The one heartening aspect was that everyone from far and near came to help. The building was surrounded not just by the Duke's employees but by villagers, visitors, and anyone at all who thought they could help to rescue some of the castle's treasures.

It has taken years to restore the castle to its former beauty and grandeur but now it is open to the public again. Its imposing square outline is broken by a massive keep which rears up from the centre, but the really eye-catching features of this neo-Gothic creation are the conical caps on the towers at each corner.

Inside the castle is a wealth of interesting features; each time I go there, something new seems to catch my eye.

The furniture, furnishings, tableware and Beauvais tapestries are rare and beautiful, and in the central hall is an impressive display of armour. I paused for a long time to gaze at the works of the great masters, portraits by Gainsborough, Hoppner, Raeburn and Ramsay, amongst others, which line the walls. Throughout, the decor bears witness to the genius of the men who created it.

Many of the treasures have historical associations. The Duke showed us a cap worn by one of his ancestors just before his execution and a dirk and sporran which had belonged to Rob Roy, one of Scotland's great adventurers. The Duke and Duchess were superb guides, both ready with a fund of anecdotes about the castle and the estate, so we were very privileged tourists.

Stuart and I spent some time exploring the gardens and the grounds beyond. The trees at Inveraray are among the finest in Scotland and there is one really massive silver fir. From the castle there are a variety of walks, tracks up both sides of Glen Shira, a picturesque waterfall to admire at the Falls of Aray, and, for the energetic, a climb up the glen to the ruins of Rob Roy's home.

Our weekend at Inveraray Castle impressed me above all with the amount of energy, enthusiasm and dedication the Duke and Duchess give to the Inveraray estate and to the interests of the town. One could not imagine a more hardworking and helpful person than Iona, the Duchess, and the Duke is one of the most charming and unassuming men I have ever met.

There are only a few Scottish castles which are small enough to be run easily and one of them, Dunderave, is just a few miles north of Inveraray. Dunderave seen from the road looks like a grey mansion house. In fact built in the sixteenth century, it is an L-shaped castle with a tower that was restored by Sir Robert Lorimer in 1912.

The owner is the Hon. Marguerite Weir, who told us a story about the castle's history which would alarm any bridegroom intent on having a rip-roaring 'stag night'. This was exactly what the last of the Macnaughtons had in mind when he was about to marry the girl he loved, the second daughter of Sir James Campbell of Ardkinglass.

The beautiful slopes of Glen Aray.

Unfortunately, his celebrations were so high-powered that Macnaughton lost track of what was happening. He woke up in the morning to find he had married the eldest daughter and not the second eldest. Furious at the trick which had been played on him, he abandoned his bride of one day and ran off to America with her sister. (I doubt *I* would have gone with him after such careless behaviour.)

Dunderave is at the head of Loch Fyne, from where there is a choice of three routes to Glasgow. Sometimes we have gone by Loch Lomond, at other times by Loch Long and on one occasion we went across the Cowal peninsula by Strachur to Dunoon. If you go by Loch Long you have the pleasure of that lovely run down the shores of the loch to Garelochhead, a pretty village on the Gare Loch, which is an arm of the Firth of Clyde.

The names of the villages on the Gare Loch — Shandon, Rhu, Helensburgh and Craigendoran — are very familiar to those who live in the west of Scotland since the circular tour of 'the three lochs' (Lomond, Long and Gare) has long been a popular Sunday outing from Glasgow.

Crossing the Cowal peninsula from Inveraray to Dunoon is another enjoyable outing amidst very different scenery. On this route, you pass through the sixty-thousand-acre Argyll Forest Park where there are mountains, flowers, and a botanic garden renowned for its flowering shrubs. After an hour's drive you find yourself at Dunoon on the Firth of Clyde. A car ferry will take you across the Firth to Gourock, which is forty-five minutes from Glasgow by car.

Each route has its own attractions, but my favourite — and the quickest road home from Inveraray and Argyll — is along the bonnie banks of Loch Lomond, the most romantic stretch of water in Scotland.

LOCH LOMOND

By yon bonnie banks and by yon bonnie braes,
Where the sun shines bright on Loch Lomond...

One of Scotland's leading men of medicine who devotes every weekend to climbing, skiing, canoeing, sailing or exploring the countryside was offered a top research job in America. He refused. I was surprised, because I had heard him praising the mountains, lakes and rivers of America. So why had he turned down the chance to work there?

'Well,' he said thoughtfully, 'in America it can take so long to get to that countryside, whereas in Glasgow it is practically on our back doorstep. I can finish work at my hospital in the centre of the city and within an hour I can be sailing on the Firth of Clyde or strolling along the banks of Loch Lomond or climbing some of the loveliest peaks in the Trossachs.'

In a few sentences he had summed up some of the advantages of living in or near Glasgow. It is a pity that they are not stressed more in documentaries on the city. These always seem to focus on the seamy side of the city and to play down its cultural aspects. After all, Glasgow was the birthplace of the Scottish National Orchestra and Scottish Opera, and the civic collection of paintings is magnificent.

Dear old Glasgow! For years the city has suffered from an image that just does not do her justice. Recently, I am glad to say, people have begun to realize that it is not only a pleasant place to live, but is very close to some of the most splendid scenery in Scotland.

It would be an insult to add Glasgow as a postscript to descriptions of Loch Lomond and the Trossachs, so let me begin with Glasgow. It is after all the largest city in Scotland, it is the city that launched me on my career and it is where I met my husband.

With memories like that, how could I ever think of Glasgow as being anything but bright and beautiful? I was not born and bred in Glasgow itself, however. My home town is Kirkintilloch,

seven miles to the north and once a fort on Antonine's Wall. My parents introduced us all — my sister Eleanor, my brothers Kenneth and Alistair, and me — to music at an early age. My father passed on to me Scottish songs his mother had taught him, and sometimes I played the piano while we all sang. When the Kirkintilloch Junior Choir was formed, we all wanted to be part of it.

The founder and conductor of the choir was a Church of Scotland minister, the Rev. John Macpherson, and his wife Meta was the accompanist. He somehow managed to train a very mixed bunch of schoolchildren from the age of six upwards to use their voices to the best of their ability and to develop a love of music. He was successful beyond his wildest dreams. The Kirkintilloch Junior Choir were invited to sing all over Britain and Europe and our concerts were frequently broadcast. One of our proudest moments was the winning of first prize at the famous Eisteddfod in Wales. Some people claimed that we were Scotland's answer to the Vienna Boys Choir. We neither knew nor cared about that — we just loved singing.

Mr Macpherson was a great believer in the biblical parable of 'using your talents'. He encouraged us to enter music festivals of all kinds. That entailed visits to the big city of Glasgow and I remember sitting on the hard seats in fear and trembling before it was my turn to go on. I have had plenty of experience of stage fright since then, but somehow nothing was quite so terrifying as those moments in my childhood when I was waiting to play the piano or to sing. On one occasion I was the forty-third competitor.

Glasgow was a great place for music festivals in those days. There was even one in Lewis's, Glasgow's biggest store, in Argyle Street. It was hardly as prestigious as the St Andrew's Halls, but oh! the joy of winning a prize that could be spent in the store.

Afterwards my mother would take me shop-

Outside the City Chambers. As a child, I thought this was the grandest building in Glasgow.

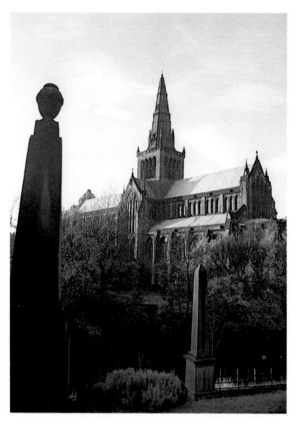

The towering Gothic structure of Glasgow Cathedral, in which I have often sung.

the day of the coronation of Queen Elizabeth II, and afterwards we went out on to the balcony and looked down on the cheering crowds in George Square — very much a night to remember!

The City Chambers occupies the entire eastern side of George Square, another of the city's landmarks. The square in summer is a riot of colourful flower displays but I loved it best that night of the coronation, and, of course, at Christmas, when the display of fairy lights and illuminated figures attracts thousands of sightseers.

The square is peopled by statues, some of them rather stern and disapproving in appearance, of Queen Victoria, Prince Albert, Sir Walter Scott, Robert Burns, William Gladstone, Robert Peel and many others. I am afraid that we are all inclined to take George Square and its statues for granted and I remember being surprised and delighted when the writer H.V. Morton commented that George Square in Glasgow and Trafalgar Square in London are the two most impressive squares in Britain.

Glasgow was founded by St Mungo in AD 543 and the site was a cluster of huts round a church called Glas Cau, the Celtic name for green place. The city's insignia ('Let Glasgow Flourish') shows the bell, the tree, the bird and the fish which represent St Mungo's miracles. Every schoolchild in Glasgow used to chant the rhyme of the motto: 'the bell that never rang, the fish that never swam, the tree that never grew and the bird that never flew.' We used to listen wide-eyed to the story of how St Mungo had brought a dead bird to life, made a frozen branch burst into flames and conjured up a fish out of the river to save a princess. To us, it was a fairy-tale, but Glasgow Cathedral is built on the site of St Mungo's church.

I came to know Glasgow Cathedral well. I visited it as a youngster and sang there with the choir, and later, when Stuart and I bought a house in Pollokshields, we found that our next-door neighbours were the minister and his wife, Dr and Mrs Morris. Glasgow Cathedral became the church I attended yet to call it simply a church seems inadequate. Dr Morris told me with justifiable pride that the cathedral is one of the most perfect examples of thirteenth-century Gothic architecture in the country. The crypt, with its fan vaulting, is one of the most splendid, not just in Britain, but in Europe. In the lower church are

ping — a great treat for me in those days. Most of all I liked going to Tam Shepherd's magic shop, where they sold fake cigarettes, squeaking cushions, biting toy dogs and repellent animals and birds that shrieked on impact. My father was always very careful where he sat down after we had been to Tam Shepherd's magic shop.

Another Glasgow treat of my childhood was going to concerts. The concerts that I loved most were the ones held in the City Chambers. The place was so magnificent it almost frightened me, yet it was a marvellous experience to walk into that vast Italian Renaissance-style building that Queen Victoria had opened in 1888.

The building has a loggia built like a Renaissance church, magnificent marble and wood panelling and two grand staircases which lead to the council chamber, reception rooms and a 110-foot-long banqueting hall lined with murals tracing the city's history.

The Kirkintilloch Choir was invited to sing to a distinguished company in the City Chambers on

Walking with my dog in the park near Glasgow
Cathedral and the Art Gallery.

the shrine of St Mungo, an ancient well and a Covenanter's tombstone.

I like the simplicity of the nave and was told that the rood screen, which has sculpted figures on it representing the seven ages of man, is very like the one in Canterbury Cathedral. There is so much to see in the cathedral: the choir, the sacristy where Oliver Cromwell once sat during a service, and the vaulted chapel known as Blacader's Aisle. But you do not need to spend hours in the cathedral to appreciate it. Even if you just step inside for a few minutes, the sheer spaciousness of it, together with the awesome height of its roof, the magnificence of the carving in wood and stone and the stained-glass windows, quite overwhelms you.

On the pulpit stands an hourglass, once used to remind the preacher not to let his sermon overrun. That, and the beautiful tapestry, designed in Edinburgh, which was unveiled by Princess Margaret in 1979, have remained in my memory ever since.

Unusual buildings in the city include Provand's Lordship (Glasgow's oldest house), the crown-topped Tolbooth Steeple and the Mercat Cross.

It is the old story. When you live in a city – and I have lived in various parts of Glasgow – you do not look at it with the eyes of a visitor, and yet, if you do, there is much to admire.

The Greek and Egyptian architecture of Alexander 'Greek' Thomson in St Vincent Street, Union Street and in Great Western Terrace is memorable for its artistry. The city's grime, I am happy to say, is being removed, and both Sauchiehall Street, the most famous street of all, and Buchanan Street have been made into pedestrian precincts.

Even as a child I marvelled at the Glasgow School of Art, designed by Charles Rennie Mackintosh. It was this building which first aroused my interest in architecture and I had plenty of time to appreciate it since I used to attend drawing lessons at the Glasgow School of Art each Saturday morning. This led to trips to the West End of the city, to the Glasgow Art Gallery which fostered my love of painting. Before and after these competitions, we were allowed to wander round the gallery and get to know great works by Botticelli, Rubens, Raphael and Rembrandt.

I knew I would never paint like these men of genius, but I would look at the work of modern painters and determine to emulate them in the next art gallery competition. Art was everywhere in Glasgow in those days. My mother used to take me to Craig's Tearooms sometimes after our shopping expeditions, and even there the walls were lined with pictures by Hornel, Wells and other members of the Scottish School.

The School of Art, where I spent many a Saturday morning learning to draw and paint.

Craig's Tearooms have gone now, but the art gallery continues to accumulate works of art and it is a great source of pride to Glaswegians to know that it houses the finest civic collection in Britain. Over the years, I have continued to visit the art gallery, and one of the pleasures of doing so is to be in that particular part of the city, Kelvingrove. In front of the gallery itself lie spacious gardens, and behind looms the spire of Glasgow University, my husband's Alma Mater. Opposite the gallery stands a building beloved of all Scottish children: the Kelvin Hall, scene of the Modern Homes exhibition, a treasure-house of free samples, the circus and the carnival.

Across the road from the art gallery is Kelvingrove Park. This place is a great favourite with amorous university students, because of its secluded walkways by the River Kelvin.

Few people outside Scotland seem to know that Glasgow has an abundance of parks, and I feel very strongly that they should. I wonder how many people who have watched scenes of Glasgow's slums or dingy tenements on television realize that the city has over seventy parks. I remember being taken on picnics to Rouken Glen, a 200-acre area of woods, waterfalls and a boating lake. Linn Park is another huge playground, the site of both Cathcart Castle ruins and the Castle Knowe, where Mary Queen of Scots watched the defeat of her forces at Langside in 1568 before leaving Glasgow for the last time. Then there is Pollok Estate, where there are not only beautiful gardens but a magnificent house filled with precious china, paintings and antiques. For a number of years I lived in a house which was only a short distance from the Pollok Estate, and I loved walking there.

Across the river Clyde is Victoria Park, where there is a fossil grove filled with fossil stumps and roots of trees which grew here some 250 million years ago. The park I know best of all is the Botanic Gardens, because it is right beside the BBC. When I left school, I went to the Royal Scottish Academy of Music in Glasgow where I trained to be a teacher, but I already felt that my future lay in performing rather than teaching. I was offered an audition by the BBC in the early 'sixties, and thereafter sang on radio and television. Gradually my name became known. *The White Heather Club* and *The Kilt is My Delight* were two series in which I appeared regularly.

By then, Glasgow's theatres were opening their doors to me, and I remember a very happy season at the old Alhambra Theatre which, sadly, no longer exists.

The turning-point came when I was in such demand as a singer that I was able to give up teaching, but still I could hardly believe my luck when I was offered a television series of my own, *Can't Help Singing*. The great advantage of this series was the fact that it was nationally networked. As people in Scottish showbusiness know, it

The Botanical Gardens, Kibble Palace, opposite the BBC.

is not so easy to get shows made in 'the regions' shown nationally. *Can't Help Singing* was followed by *Moira Anderson Sings* and it was an enormous thrill for me when this series appeared in the ratings.

To present *Stars on Sunday,* which I did for two years, I had to go to Yorkshire, but all my other television series were filmed in Scotland. I came to know the BBC studios in Queen Margaret Drive very well, and had ample opportunity to explore the nearby Botanic Gardens.

Before and after a television session, I would walk round the gardens to calm my nerves. There are flowers blooming there throughout the year and even on the coldest day in winter I could go into the Kibble Palace, a domed greenhouse where there is a winter garden, or admire the orchids and other beautiful flowers in the hothouses.

I think it was during one of those walks in the Botanic Gardens that Evelyn Elliot, a BBC presenter, persuaded me to come to her house and meet Stuart Macdonald, a medical colleague of her husband's who had been best man at their wedding. Stuart and I married within the year.

The public parks and gardens of Glasgow were not its only joy for me when I was young. I was equally enchanted by the city's docks. Those were the days when 'Clyde-built' was a phrase which made every Glaswegian proud to belong to a famous shipbuilding city. It was always a great moment for us to watch great liners being launched, and I doubt if anyone in Glasgow will ever forget the launching of the *QE2.*

Long before that great ship was launched in 1968, I had been initiated into our own special launchings: the trips 'doon the watter'. The 'watter' in this case always means the river Clyde, but no phrase can conjure up those magical moments in my childhood when we stepped aboard the steamer at the Broomielaw. As the boat moved away from its berth, we crowded excitedly on deck so that we could watch the river ferries and see the giant cranes loading and unloading their cargoes. Being within earshot of the busy shipyards we used to wave frantically to the riveters, perched like mountain goats on the hilltops of the ships they were working on, and cheer loudly when the riveters waved back.

Once we spotted Dumbarton Rock, we knew open water was ahead. Soon we would come to

Greenock, Gourock (the 'tail of the Bank'), Dunoon, and Rothesay on the island of Bute. Sometimes we caught the train from Glasgow to Gourock. The steamer from Gourock would sail to Kirn, Dunoon, Innellan, Rothesay, then round the Kyles of Bute calling at Tighnabruaich, Tarbert and Ardrishaig.

The Firth of Clyde is at its most colourful and lively during the Clyde Fortnight, when yachts gather for competitions and the blue waters of the Firth are painted with white, red, blue and yellow sails and spinnakers.

If the trip 'doon the watter' was one of my most cherished childhood treats, a trip 'up the waters of Loch Lomond' was another. We were all immensely proud of Loch Lomond. Was it not the largest stretch of inland water in Britain, and the most beautiful loch in the country?

In 1746 when Bonnie Prince Charlie's cause was lost and he was once again fleeing from his enemies, two of his loyal soldiers were imprison-

ed in Carlisle. Ironically, at the very hour one of them was to be released, the other was to be executed. 'Loch Lomond' is the elegy of the man who was about to die. He recalls the bonnie banks and braes of Loch Lomond where he used to meet his sweetheart, then the day of parting:

I mind when we parted in yon shady glen,
On the steep steep side of Ben Lomond...

He knows he will never meet her there again.

The doomed prisoner's only consolation is that he will reach Scotland before his friend, because at the moment of dying his spirit will take the 'low road' straight back to his birthplace and he will be there immediately, whereas his friend will have to tramp many miles over 'the high road' before he reaches his home.

The song's aura of romance and history heightened our sense of anticipation as we travelled to the loch. I could hardly contain my excitement when the train from Glasgow reached Balloch, at

Loch Lomond's most southerly tip, where *The Maid of the Loch* would be waiting to take us on a twenty-two-mile cruise.

The loch itself varies in width from five miles to a mere five hundred yards, so we would have every chance on our cruise to admire the beauty of its banks and braes and see the islands, over thirty of them, which make Loch Lomond such a picturesque stretch of water.

The first of the islands you come to is Inchmurrin. The Earls of Lennox built a stronghold there but could not prevent their heirs being exiled, imprisoned and executed by James I. We used to look at the ivy-encrusted ruins of the old castle and wonder if the jackdaws there were black ghosts come to haunt the castle.

Ghosts there could well have been, for we could look westwards from Inchmurrin, beyond the banks of Loch Lomond, to Glen Fruin where the Colquhouns were massacred by the Mac-Gregors. The MacGregors held sway over the

Rowing on Loch Lomond, aided and abetted by my dog Jimmy.

land between Loch Lomond and Loch Katrine, but a dispute arose over this territory between them and the Colquhouns. When the clan chief of Colquhoun killed two MacGregors who strayed on to his land, the MacGregor clan swooped down and massacred the Colquhouns.

Rob Roy MacGregor, hero of Sir Walter Scott's novel *Rob Roy,* was well known to us. In real life he was an outlaw and a blackmailer, but Sir Walter Scott had romanticized him so much that we saw him as a Robin Hood figure.

When Scott was researching his facts about Rob Roy, he stayed at Ross Priory, a headland on the eastern shore of Loch Lomond, and this was one of the landmarks we looked for after passing the islets of Creinch and Torrinch.

Between Balmaha on the east side of Loch Lomond and Luss on the west, islands are scattered like mounds of moss: Inch Fad, Inch Moan, Inch Tavannach, Inch Connachan, Inch Cruin, Inch Loanig and Inch Galbraith.

After Luss, the loch becomes narrower and the scenery more dramatic, with high hills crowding the shoreline. One of the places where the *Maid of the Loch* used to stop was Rowardennan, well known for its youth hostel and its proximity to Ben Lomond. The mountain is over 3,000 feet high, but you can walk to the top in two to three hours. From the summit you have a bird's-eye view of island-studded Loch Lomond, the Argyllshire hills and the Grampian mountains.

Once we were married, Stuart and I made many trips to Loch Lomond by car. The road along its west bank must be one of the most beautiful in Britain. Trees form archways through which you can glimpse its green islands, white cottages and glinting blue water, never more than a few yards from the hedgerows.

Quite often we stopped at Luss, one of the prettiest villages in Scotland, where the wooded hillsides slope gently down to a cluster of cottages covered in roses and greenery. We would wander along the shore and then drive up the lochside to Ardlui, which is right at the northern tip of the loch and a couple of miles from the entrance to lovely Glen Falloch. After seeing the Falls of Falloch we would lie in the heather gazing up at the mountains all around.

Sometimes, for a change, we would make a round-trip and drive halfway up Loch Lomond to Tarbet on the west bank. To the east of Tarbet lies Arrochar at the head of Loch Long. At this point, Loch Lomond and Loch Long incline towards each other like two sides of a triangle. They are separated by a mere two-mile stretch of roadway. In the thirteenth century the Norsemen used to drag their ships across this isthmus from one loch to the other so that they could attack the interior of Scotland.

Further from Glasgow, but still only an hour's drive away, are the Trossachs. The word 'trossachs' means 'bristly country', and if you look down from an aeroplane at the densely wooded hills and valleys between Loch Achray and Loch Katrine, you can see how apt the name is.

The most popular route to the Trossachs from Glasgow is through Milngavie and Blanefield to Aberfoyle, another gateway to the Trossachs. Three miles east of Aberfoyle is the only lake in Scotland, the lake of Menteith, a lovely spot and a favourite venue for water-skiers.

An alternative road from Aberfoyle leads you eastwards along Loch Ard and Loch Chon to Stronachlachar near the head of Loch Katrine. Another well-loved route to the Trossachs is from Callander. Callander is a good starting-point because it is only forty miles from Glasgow (and fifty from Edinburgh). Television viewers all over Britain came to know it well since it formed the setting for the long-running television series *Dr Finlay's Casebook.*

From the top of Ben Ledi, which overlooks Callander, you can see Ben Lawers and, forty miles to the south-east, the Forth Bridge.

The author J. M. Barrie had links with the Roman Camp Hotel. Stuart and I love going out there for an early lunch, then taking the road along Loch Venacher to Brig o'Turk, a pretty little village which is popular with artists. I am always hoping to stumble on an undiscovered masterpiece, so I insist on stopping whenever I see pictures displayed in a shop window.

At lovely Loch Achray blue mountains and water are a perfect foil for the hazels, oaks and silver birches lining the road. Turner is probably not the only artist to have painted that scene.

Whichever way you travel in this glorious area, you find natural beauty at its most stunning. With such marvellous scenery on our 'back doorstep', who can blame us, or the eminent Scottish physician, for staying loyal to Scotland's largest city?

Luss Harbour, Loch Lomond, at the mouth of the Glen of Luss.

MY LOVE IS LIKE
A RED, RED ROSE

O my love is like a red, red rose,
That's newly sprung in June...

'My love is like a red, red rose' could not be a more appropriate song to introduce reminiscences of Grampian and Royal Deeside since Aberdeen, on Scotland's north-east coast, has become famous for its roses, and since it was in Aberdeen and Royal Deeside that my own love affair blossomed one summer. I became engaged to Stuart just before taking up my first full summer season at His Majesty's Theatre.

That summer when I was newly engaged is one I will never forget. Stuart used to come up from Glasgow every weekend and when we were not seeing the sights of the city we would motor out to all the romantic spots in Royal Deeside.

Looking back, I realize now how fortunate we were to spend that summer in a place like Aberdeen, for although it is the third largest city in Scotland, it has a compact charm which makes exploration easy. If you are travelling from the south, you can enter the city by crossing the King George VI Bridge which spans the Dee. Aberdeen lies between two rivers, the Don and the Dee. Further up the latter stands the Bridge of Dee. That seven-ribbed structure has coats of arms on its piers and abutments and when I first saw it I was much impressed by its elegance. It was here that Aberdeen's Royalists fought with the Covenanters. The Royalists lost and the bridge was damaged, but it was later restored and now it stands as a graceful reminder of the city's past.

His Majesty's Theatre, where I was singing that summer, is on Rosemount Viaduct beside the public library and the South Church, St Mark's. The Aberdonians jokingly refer to the three buildings standing side by side as 'Education, Salvation and Damnation'.

I very much doubt that our show at His Majesty's could have been the cause of anyone's damnation. Those were the days when a night at the theatre meant songs, dances and innocuous sketches suitable for young and old alike. I took part in the sketches as well and in one of them I played a doctor's wife. Stuart tells me he used to watch that scene very carefully to see how I measured up.

My main reason for being there, however, was to sing. It seemed in keeping with my romantic mood that for one song, 'So In Love', I was perched on a crescent moon which floated across the stage. That was, at least, the general idea, but on occasions the mechanism would develop a fault and I would 'float' across the stage in fits and starts like a learner driver.

Near the theatre is the city's art gallery, where the works of Sir William MacTaggart, George Jamesone and many other celebrated Scottish artists are well represented. Everyone at the gallery was friendly when Stuart and I visited it at weekends, and I remember one man telling us the story of James Cassie, a local artist who made the famous Aberdonian boast: 'There's Jamesone, Dyce and Phillip - tak' awa' Aberdeen and twal' mile roon it and faur are ye?'

The man laughed heartily at this joke and we laughed politely with him although we had not the faintest idea what he meant. We were discovering by then that the local Aberdonian patois sometimes needs translation. For example, 'quine' is a girl and 'fit' is commonly used for what. 'Faur' means where, and roughly translated that famous Aberdonian boast means 'Without Aberdeen's artists, what would be worth seeing?'

I can understand why James Cassie was so proud of Aberdeen, because it certainly is a lovely city. Near the theatre the buildings, including the Old Infirmary, the Cowdray Hall and the war memorial, are faced in grey and pink granite. Many of them have coloured domes, too. When you hear people talking of Aberdeen as the 'granite city', you imagine a dull, lifeless place,

The river Clunie at Braemar - a haven of peace and tranquillity.

Aberdeen's magnificent harbour and a panorama of the granite city.

but when the sun sparkles on that granite, you can understand why one poet referred to it as the 'glitter of mica' and Lewis Grassic Gibbon talked of Aberdeen's 'shining mail'.

The granite used to be taken from the quarry at Rubislaw, and even though that enormous vein has been exhausted, new buildings in the city still have the 'glitter of mica' because there are granite chips in the cement blocks which are now used for building.

You can see the gleam of granite almost everywhere in Aberdeen, particularly in Union Street, which runs a mile from east to west across the city. I used to shop in Union Street, and I often paused to look up at the buildings above the shops or to explore some of the side streets.

Castlegate, where Lord Byron used to play as a boy, is the centre of Aberdeen. In the Town House you can see the charters which William the Lionheart granted to the city in the twelfth century and the famous charter granted by Robert the Bruce.

I was fascinated by the Mercat Cross in Castlegate, because there are portraits on this circular arcade of all the Scottish sovereigns from James I to James VII. Not all of them were as compassionate as Mary Queen of Scots, who wept when she was forced to watch the execution of Sir John Gordon at this spot. Sir John was beheaded by a guillotine called 'the Maiden'.

One day I walked from Castlegate to Shiprow and visited one of the oldest buildings in the city, Provost Ross's House, which is now a maritime museum. Another old house which has been lovingly restored is Provost Skene's House, a

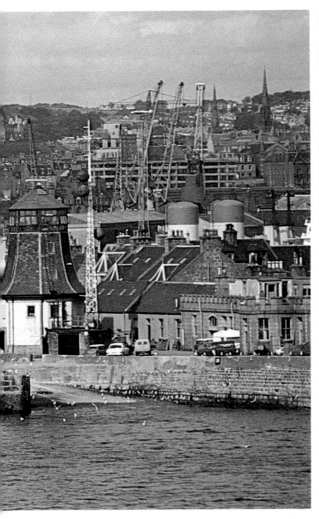

in the mornings and afternoons we had time to visit the city's monuments, museums, and churches: St Andrew's Cathedral in King Street and St Nicholas Church, regarded as the 'Mither Kirk' (mother church) and containing the largest carillon of bells in Great Britain.

If the weather was fine, we went for walks, stopping frequently to admire the beautiful gardens which front some of the granite houses. Aberdonians have always seemed to me more interested in flowers than most other town-dwellers and, indeed, horticulturists have said that the private gardens in Aberdeen are second to none.

There are roses in most of these gardens and the main roads of the city are lined with flowers. The District Council decided some time ago that roses were much easier to keep up than patches of grass, and as a result of their efforts in the parks and thoroughfares, Aberdeen has won the 'Britain in Bloom' title a number of times. Aberdeen even has a garden that was specially created for the blind, so that they can smell the exquisite blooms they cannot see.

Seaton Park was another favourite venue for us on a Saturday afternoon. Since the park is just fifteen minutes from the theatre, we had plenty of time to wander through the woods to the deep gorge of the Don. Here we could look down on the old Brig o' Balgownie which spans the Don in a spectacular Gothic arch. The bridge is said to be one of the oldest in Scotland.

Above Seaton Park is another landmark, St Machar's Cathedral. St Machar chose this spot to found his church because he had been commanded to find a place where the river bent like a bishop's crozier. There has been a church on this spot since the sixth century, and the present structure dates from 1357.

Among our favourite haunts in Aberdeen were the seafront and the dunes. The sandy beach, which stretches for miles along the coastline, is a great place for walking and as the weather that summer was very warm the cool sea breezes were wonderfully refreshing.

We loved going to the harbour early in the morning when the fish were being auctioned and it saddens me to hear how much the fishing industry has declined since those days. For centuries, fishing was the source of Aberdeen's prosperity, but now the oil industry has taken over.

seventeenth-century building which is now a museum of civic and domestic life.

These old granite houses are extremely impressive, but for sheer artistry in granite it is difficult to beat the splendid university buildings. The original University of Aberdeen was founded in 1494, but the College Chapel and King's College with its crown tower were not built until the beginning of the sixteenth century. In 1593 Marischal College, in Broad Street, was founded as a rival to King's College. The fretted pinnacles and the intricate sculpting of its elaborate facade are quite breathtaking, and at one time it was the second largest granite building in the world (the Escorial in Madrid being largest of all). It was one of the first places I pointed out to Stuart when I took him on a tour of the city.

Apart from Saturday evenings, when I was on stage, my weekends that summer were free. So

Strangely enough, although everyone associates oil with Aberdeen, the visitor to the city is hardly aware of it since no oil comes ashore here. It is only when you go to the harbour and see the constant traffic of the brightly painted supply boats or catch a glimpse of a rig moored on the horizon that you remember that Aberdeen is the oil capital of Europe. It has affected the city, of course. There is a general atmosphere of prosperity, and the men working on the rigs come back after a fortnight on duty with good wages to spend. Naturally there have been difficulties, but Aberdeen seems to have come to terms with the oil industry since so many people are benefiting from it. However, one reflection of Aberdeen's affluence is that property prices have soared, and

Exploring Royal Deeside made a welcome break from my summer show in Aberdeen.

young couples in Aberdeen find that a great problem. But Aberdonians never lose their pawky sense of humour. One of the things I like about them is that they make fun of everything, especially their (ill-founded) reputation for meanness over money. When someone exclaimed at the narrowness of a small door in one of the rooms of a flat, the Aberdonian owner remarked cheerfully: 'Och, yon's a real Aberdeen door — ye canna get much oot of it!'

We were often reluctant to tear ourselves away from Aberdeen's beaches and parks on a Saturday afternoon, but the show had to go on. The Saturday-night audience at His Majesty's Theatre was always the biggest of the week. Once I was at the theatre, I tried to forget about everything except what I had to do on stage, although frequently Stuart would be waiting in the wings.

After the show, we would have a meal and dis-

cuss our plans for the next day. If you use Aberdeen as a base, the opportunities for sightseeing are superb. To the west rise Britain's highest ranges of mountains, the Grampians and Cairngorms. Many of Stuart's friends are climbers and they have described to me the exhilaration of reaching the high summits. In winter, under the snow, the mountains become a holiday playground for skiers. Aviemore and Glenshee attract enthusiasts from England and Europe. Although I do not ski myself, I am very proud, as a patriotic Scot, of the foresight of those who developed the Aviemore complex and made it the finest ski centre in Britain.

Having just called the Aviemore 'the finest', I find I want to use another superlative about our fishing facilities. To the north-west of Aberdeen is the Spey valley, through which runs the river Spey. The Spey abounds with both salmon and superb sea trout. Aberdeen caters for golfers, too. There is said to be a golf course for every day of the month within easy reach of Aberdeen. The one with the best view is probably Balnagownie, where the panorama of city, sea, river and mountain can have few equals. We often went up there just to enjoy the view.

Saturday mornings and afternoons passed all too quickly, but Sundays were free to be enjoyed and we often drove out to Deeside.

Deeside deserves to be called 'royal'. It has enjoyed royal patronage since the twelfth century, although it was really Queen Victoria and Prince Albert who established Deeside as a royal residence. Since then, successive royal families have used it as a summer home. Every year in August the Royal Yacht *Britannia* sails up the Dee and docks at the Atlantic Wharf, where the Royal Family disembark to begin their holiday.

Many people have taken the royal road along the banks of the river Dee from Aberdeen to Braemar and Stuart and I came to know it well that summer. We usually set off early so that we could have a long, leisurely day and perhaps visit a castle or two on the way. In fact there are more castles concentrated in this area than in any other part of the country I know.

Our usual route from Aberdeen was through Cults and Culter. In the thirteenth century Culter was divided into two parishes: Maryculter and Peterculter, named respectively after the church on the south side of the Dee dedicated to the

Loch Avon, high in the Cairngorms, in its dramatic setting near Aviemore.

Virgin Mary and after the church on the north side dedicated to St Peter. Beyond Peterculter there are several castles. First of all you come to Drum, an imposing granite mansion belonging to the National Trust. Some of its walls are twelve feet thick, and on its barrel-vaulted ceiling are displayed a series of shields, each bearing a coat of arms. Drum also features a thirteenth-century tower house.

Five miles farther on is one of the most famous castles in Scotland, Crathes Castle. It stands in a commanding position on the north slopes of the river Dee in over five hundred acres of ground, in which there is a lovely walled garden — as well as beautiful flowers, shrubs and trees. I love the warm pink stone of Crathes Castle and its ornate architecture, bristling with towers, turrets and gables.

Crathes Castle has a ghost known as the Green Lady, who used to be seen flitting along the corridors. As if to substantiate the story of this ghost, the skeletons of a woman and child were found behind one of the castle's fireplaces in Victorian times. Crathes Castle itself goes back much further, of course — to 1323, when Robert the Bruce granted a 'horn of tenure' to Alexander Burnard. The horn, made of fluted ivory, four bands of gilt and three crystals, is one of the most treasured possessions of the Burnetts of Ley.

The Green Lady's room on the third floor has eye-catching ceiling decorations painted by Jacobean artists. The bedroom ceilings on the second floor are just as brightly painted. It is remarkable that the colour is so vibrant when you consider that these ceilings lay concealed under a layer of plaster until 1877. The names of the rooms are interesting in themselves: the Chamber of the Nine Muses and the Chamber of the Nine Nobles. The latter portrays three Christian champions, three Old Testament heroes and three pagan heroes. One poet praised each hero

in a rhyme and then asked the reader: 'Gude redar tell me or you pass/Whilk of these myn maist valiant was?' (which of these heroes was the bravest?).

When we left the bedrooms, we decided to take a closer look at the great hall of the castle. I wanted to spend a little time studying the paintings of Jamesone, the father of Scottish portrait painters. We had time not only to see Crathes but also to take a look at Tilquhillie Castle, opposite Crathes on the south bank of the Dee, and to wander through the ruins of Cluny-Crichton Castle near Banchory.

Since the advent of North Sea oil, which has made Aberdeen so busy, Banchory has become a very popular residential area. One of the prettiest spots on Deeside, it lies eighteen miles outside the city. If it was light enough when we arrived there, we would go for a walk on the golf course or visit the spectacular salmon leap at Brig o' Feugh before going on to see friends.

After our day on Deeside, we would return to

Left Crathes Castle, Grampian, from the grounds.
Below One of its bedrooms, showing the painted ceiling.

Aberdeen and I would prepare for another week at His Majesty's. As the days flew past, I would begin to think of the places we could explore on the Saturday and Sunday to come. When we visited the castles in the lower reaches of the Dee, we decided it was time to go farther along the royal road.

From Banchory the A93 leads you along the banks of the river Dee to Aboyne. Aboyne is a pretty little Highland village with a ruined castle and a backdrop of woods and hills, but it has become most celebrated for its Highland Games. The Highland Games at Aboyne, Ballater and Braemar are among Deeside's biggest attractions.

Originally, games of this sort were started by the Highland chiefs so that they could select the strongest men for their bodyguards. The Games are still a test for the strongest men, but now women sometimes participate as well. There are athletic events of all kinds, but the Highland Games are much more than a local Olympics. The pageantry of the pipe bands and the colourful competitions for Highland dancing and piping give the games a festive atmosphere which you would never find at the Olympics.

And of course, it is only at the Highland Games that you will find an event such as tossing the caber. I use the word 'event' advisedly because I am inclined to think some of the competitors have acquired their dramatic huffing and puffing technique at the Old Vic.

Queen Victoria's favourite holiday home, Balmoral Castle, now the Royal Family's summer residence, attracts many visitors. The royal road to Deeside runs through Aboyne, Dinnet and Ballater. A train used to run from Aberdeen to Ballater, and I remember having watched countless cinema newsreels of the Royal Family alighting at Ballater Station before going to Balmoral. The train service has been discontinued, but the road from Aberdeen is very good.

Ballater, like Balmoral, is a place that tempts you to stay awhile. The village itself is set in a beautiful area in which you could spend weeks exploring. Queen Victoria loved the long valley of Glen Muick, south-west of Ballater. In her Highland Journal of 1849, she describes Loch Muick as having wild, grand Highland scenery and says that she had 'various scrambles in and out of the boat and along the shore, saw three hawks and caught seventy trout.'

I would love to have met Queen Victoria. What a marvellous lady, ready for anything!

Queen Victoria was even stout-hearted enough to ascend Lochnagar, the 3,786-foot mountain which dominates the skyline in this part of Deeside. Lochnagar inspired Lord Byron to write:

Over the crags that are wild and majestic,
the steep frowning glories of dark Lochnagar...

Lochnagar can indeed be dark. Some corries on the mountain are so dangerous that they have never been climbed. But there is an accessible route to the top, and this was the one taken by Queen Victoria, from Balmoral.

She makes light of her achievement in her journals, commenting casually that when she got off her pony, she had to climb over steep stones before she reached the top. The ascent took her party four hours and there was mist everywhere. But Lochnagar made a deep impression on her. Later in her journal, she refers to it as 'the jewel of all the mountains here'.

Her great-great-grandson, Prince Charles, wrote a story about it, *The Old Man of Lochnagar*, which made Lochnagar world-famous.

The road from Ballater to Braemar was one of our favourite routes that summer. When you leave Ballater and round the huge granite heights of Craigendarroch, you find yourself in pleasantly wooded country with the silvery Dee always in sight, and always beckoning you onwards. Sometimes we stopped and had a picnic by the river and once we parked the car on the opposite bank at Abergeldie Castle. In a later chapter, 'The Birks of Aberfeldy', I mention that some people thought the poet had meant to write 'the birks of Abergeldie'. I can see why: the birches at Abergeldie are some of the finest I have seen anywhere. These graceful trees have an air of fragility which strongly appeals to me.

Soon after Abergeldie, you come to Crathie church, an unpretentious granite building with a red roof and a little spire. It has become well known because the Royal family worship there when they are staying at Balmoral. Queen Victoria helped meet the cost of building the kirk, even organizing a bazaar at Balmoral to raise money for it. Her stallholders were princes, princesses and duchesses.

Balmoral Castle is just across the river from Crathie. It was Prince Albert, Queen Victoria's consort, who bought the Balmoral estate in 1852. He hired the city architect of Aberdeen to design a new castle of two separate blocks of buildings connected by wings with a massive turreted tower at one end. Naturally Prince Albert wanted the castle built in the hand-dressed granite which is such a feature of Grampian and Deeside, and today the contrast between the silver granite and the soft green of the surrounding countryside makes Balmoral more than worthy of its Gaelic name, 'majestic dwelling'.

Prince Albert bequeathed Balmoral to Queen Victoria, who called it her 'dear Paradise' and

used it as her holiday home long after his death.

On the ground floor of Balmoral are the drawing room, dining room, billiard room and library. The private rooms of the Royal Family are on the first floor, but people who have been guests at Balmoral say its outstanding features are the grand staircase and sixty-eight-foot ballroom. The ballroom is open to the public in the absence of the Court, as are the grounds, superbly situated on a curve of the river Dee. Wherever you look, there are roses, woods, glens and mountains, including Lochnagar.

Seven miles to the west of Balmoral is Braemar. Braemar holds its celebrated Highland Games in September while the Queen is in residence, and this is the time of year when Deeside becomes crowded with tourists.

Deeside was not crowded that summer when I explored it with Stuart, and we had peace in which to explore the wonderful countryside.

We had intended to wait for a year before we were married — at least, that is what I thought we should do when I began my summer season in Aberdeen, but the granite city, strangely enough, must have melted my heart.

In any event, it was a mere month after leaving Aberdeen that we were married — at Alloway Parish Church, Ayrshire.

Throwing the hammer at the Highland Games, Aberdeen.

YE BANKS AND BRAES
O' BONNIE DOON

Ye banks and braes o' bonnie Doon,
How can ye bloom sae fresh and fair?

'Ye Banks and Braes o' Bonnie Doon' is a song that has a special meaning for me because it is set in Ayrshire, the south-west corner of Scotland known as the Burns Country.

The magic of this particular ballad, the beguiling beauty of the countryside and the legends surrounding Scotland's national bard draw thousands of people every year from all over the world to view the banks and braes of bonnie Doon, and to visit Burns' birthplace, a two-roomed cottage at Alloway in Ayrshire.

This is surely one of the most romantic spots in the whole of Britain. The Grecian columns of the Burns monument are set amidst flower-filled gardens on the banks of the river Doon; the river itself is spanned by the Brig o' Doon, the fifteenth-century bridge immortalized by Burns in his poem 'Tam o' Shanter'.

In the poem Tam, the hero, has spent a hard day drinking with his friend Souter Johnnie. By the time he decides he had better go home to Alloway and face his wife he knows she will be 'gathering her brow like gathering storm, nursing her wrath to keep it warm'. Fearfully he looks out at the dark rain-lashed street through an alcoholic haze, and leaving the shelter of the inn he mounts his old grey mare. As he rides along he sees 'bogles' in every bush, and when he stops at the ruins of the church at Alloway his bemused eyes catch sight of the Devil himself dancing with his witches and warlocks.

Tam foolishly stays to watch and in his drunken stupor forgets to stay silent. When he shouts his admiration for one comely witch, he suddenly finds the whole fiendish pack chasing after him. Tam spurs on his grey mare. He knows that his only hope of safety is to reach the old bridge over the river Doon, because witches will not cross running water. Just as he gets to the bridge, one of them snatches off his grey mare's tail, but Tam manages to reach the other side.

The high-arched bridge over the river Doon is still there today, part of the picturesque scene which includes landscaped gardens, the ruins of Alloway Kirk and, alongside, the present Parish Church in which I was married in 1967.

The cottage in which Robert Burns was born, on 25 January 1759, is nearby, a thatched, two-roomed 'auld clay biggin'. Unfortunately it was not very well built, for on the night the poet was born the gable end of the house fell in. In his poem 'There was a lad was born in Kyle', Burns recalls:

Twas then a blast of Jan'war win, blew hansel in on
        Robin.

Now, of course, the cottage is fully restored and has become a mecca for all Burns-lovers. By any standards it is an interesting example of a typical eighteenth-century working-class home. There are pots hanging by the fire, an old dresser holding china plates and a huge grandfather clock which dwarfs every other item of furniture in the room, including the hole-in-the-wall box bed in the kitchen where Burns was born.

In the garden at the back, there is a museum with a collection of Burns relics, including original manuscripts and the poet's family Bible. Of more recent vintage is the pen which the Queen used to sign the visitors' book when she came to the cottage in 1956.

The British are not the only admirers of Robert Burns. I have been asked to sing his songs by people all over the world. Indeed, I once had a request for 'Ae Fond Kiss' from a Chinese in Hong Kong. (This was not a proposition: it was the song he wanted.)

Since an increasing number of visitors come to the Burns Country and Burns' birthplace each year, Kyle and Carrick District Council decided they had to do something more to satisfy the curiosity of all his admirers. In 1977, they built a new Land o' Burns Centre. It has an audio-visual

On the Brig o' Doon, Tam o' Shanter's route to safety in the poem that bears his name.

theatre show, projecting the life of the Bard and his times, as well as memorabilia of every kind: records, books, songs, poems and souvenirs.

As I have lived in Alloway and was educated at Ayr Academy it was a special thrill when I was invited to open this fine new centre. Burns described the county town in these words:

Auld Ayr, wham ne'er a town surpasses
For honest men and bonny lasses.

(Early in my singing career, I was actually billed in a concert programme as 'A breath of fresh Ayr' — an embarrassing description to live up to, or live down.)

Robert Burns was baptised in Ayr's 'Auld Parish Kirk' and that is where he worshipped — probably in fear and trembling. In the eighteenth century, the church in Scotland was dominated by ministers and elders threatening their congregations with hellfire and brimstone. Sin could be anything from telling lies to what used to be called fornication. The culprits were made to sit on a stool in front of the whole congregation whilst they were publicly rebuked.

Burns had to suffer this humiliation and so had some of the girls he had led astray in the cornfields near his father's farm. He endured it unwillingly and later in his life his scathing verses made mockery of the stern Calvinism of the age which blighted so many lives.

In lighter vein, Burns wrote about another well-known landmark in Ayr: the two bridges, one old, one new. In his poem 'The Brigs o' Ayr', the old bridge taunts the new, claiming that 'I'll be a brig when you're a shapeless cairn'. The poet's prophecy came true when the new bridge was washed away in a storm. It was replaced, but I do not think it would dare to have an argument with the Auld Brig, which is still standing.

Burns' favourite 'howff' in Ayr was the inn later known as the Tam o' Shanter Inn, now a museum. If you pass through Ayr today, you cannot miss it. Few other taverns in Britain can have such a quaint entrance. China heads of Tam and his drinking crony Souter Johnnie are situated one on each side of the front door, and above the lamp-lit sign is a picture showing Tam mounting the old grey mare which took him from Ayr over the bridge of Doon to the safety of Alloway.

Looking back at my childhood, I realize I owe a great debt to my old school, Ayr Academy. The

Above Haunted Alloway Kirk, where Robert Burns' father is buried. *Right* At Burns' Cottage, a stark 'auld clay biggin'.

teachers tried to make us see beneath the surface to the poet's art, philosophy and wisdom.

Every year the school had Burns concerts, competitions and a splendid supper, and as a result we all grew up with this dark, handsome stranger as a friendly ghost at our elbow. I remember one year we gave a recital for Samuel Marshak who translated all of Burns' poems into Russian. Years later when I was singing at a Burns Supper, I felt very moved when the Russian ambassador to Britain presented me with a copy of Marshak's edition of Burns.

If you visit the centre at Alloway you will no doubt see the official tribute to Burns the poet, but if you explore the fair country of Ayrshire a little farther, you will begin to appreciate Burns the man. This Burns heritage trail will take you through the little villages and farms and bring you closer to the people.

When Burns was eight years old, his father acquired the lease of a farm, Mount Oliphant, which stands on high ground outside Alloway. The house is a white stone cottage, typical of Scotland, and particularly of the Ayrshire coast where many such dwellings have survived.

Some of these holdings are still being farmed; others have been bought as holiday homes because they are secluded and peaceful and command marvellous views of the Ayrshire coast and the Arran hills across the water.

Almost everywhere in Ayrshire seems to have some association with Burns. The village of Kirkoswald, on the Maybole road, is where Burns went to learn mensuration and surveying, and is also where many of the characters in his poems come from. Tam o'Shanter was Douglas Graham of Shanter farm. Souter Johnnie was the Kirkoswald souter or cobbler, and at Souter Johnnie's cottage there is a collection of the tools of his trade which were used in his lifetime.

That is one of the things that appeals to me about Burns: the characters in his poems were real people, not figments of his imagination.

At Tarbolton, you will find out about the debating club Robert Burns formed when the family moved to Lochlea farm nearby. This was for young men who wished to improve their manners and social behaviour. You can still see the plaque on the wall of a house in the village: Tarbolton Bachelors' Club.

It could be argued, though, that Scotland's national bard learned the social graces too well:

Green grow the rashes o
Green grow the rashes o
The sweetest hours that e'er I spend
Are spent among the lasses o.

His life story reads like a catalogue of entanglements and conquests worthy of Don Giovanni. No wonder fathers in Tarbolton locked up their daughters when the good-looking young farmer passed through their village. On the other hand, without such experience how could the young poet have written such memorable love songs as 'My luv is like a red, red rose' and 'Ae Fond Kiss'? These express perfectly the mingled pain and ecstasy of love, and I never tire of hearing them.

Meanwhile, Burns was being trained by his father to become a farmer. When Burns Senior decided to grow flax he sent his son to Irvine, where he was initiated into the mysteries of heckling (dressing the flax to prepare it for spinning).

The poet had neither aptitude nor liking for the work and must have been relieved when the

heckling house burnt down. As far as he was concerned, the best thing to come out of his sojourn at Irvine was the encouragement given to him by a young sea captain, Richard Brown. One day while strolling together in Eglinton woods outside the town Burns read some of his poems aloud and Brown was so impressed that he urged him to try to get them published. In Eglinton woods today you can see a plaque commemorating this meeting, which was to prove so important for Burns.

By the time Burns returned to Lochlea farm his father's health had deteriorated. When he died, Burns managed to salvage something from the wreckage and to lease Mossgiel farm near Mauchline. Mauchline is a place I know well as I taught there after graduating from the Royal Scottish Academy of Music. I used to go to Poosie Nansie's for lunch each day. Burns patronized that inn too, when he lived at Mossgiel, and Poosie Nansie was the wife of the innkeeper. The inn became the setting for Burns' cantata 'The Jolly Beggars'.

While he was farming at Mossgiel Burns met Jean Armour ('Bonnie Jean'). She was just one in a long line of conquests, but had the distinction of being the one he eventually married.

Burns commemorated his birth in the song 'There was a lad was born in Kyle'. Kyle used to be the central portion of Ayrshire; Cunninghame lay to the north, Carrick to the south. I am always amused by the old rhyme which tries to sum up the whole south-west region of Scotland in four lines:

Kyle for a man (the Bard)
Carrick for a coo (cattle)
Cunninghame for butter and cheese
and Galloway for 'oo (wool).

No one is quite sure where the name Kyle came from; it usually signifies an isthmus of land, but another theory is that Kyle was derived from King Cole or Coil, a Pictish king who was buried in this district.

I feel that too many people have tried to depict Burns' life as a hard and dreary affair, but in fact once the Kilmarnock edition of his poems was published in 1786 (the Edinburgh edition followed in 1787) he had achieved the recognition and fame that were his due.

But there is more to Ayrshire than Burns.

The Ayrshire countryside, near Alloway, unchanged since Burns' own day.

Along the coastline are dotted famous holiday resorts, the most important of these being Ayr, with its splendid beach and busy harbour. Other places such as Troon, Fairlie and Largs have their own attractions and have kept their popularity through the years.

Fairlie is a little seaside town, with Kelburn Castle a short distance to the north. The castle has belonged to the Boyles of Kelburn (the family name) since the twelfth century. The 1st Earl of Glasgow was created in 1703. Next to the castle is Kelburn golf course. There is a story that one day the current Earl of Glasgow was rebuked by a stranger for going into the clubhouse improperly dressed, and was asked if he did not own a tie. 'Yes,' he replied crisply, 'and I own the golf course as well.'

For me, Fairlie was THE PIER in large capital letters. It was from there you could catch a ferry to Millport on the island of Greater Cumbrae. Millport, with its sandy beaches and boating facilities, meant summer sunshine and a reprieve from school.

Further down the Ayrshire coast is Ardrossan which, like Fairlie, is best known for its pier. Steamers leave from here for the island of Arran.

For many Scotsmen, summer is above all the time for golf, and Ayrshire is particularly fortunate in having three championship golf courses: Troon, Prestwick and Turnberry. All three are seaside courses with fine turf and beautiful views. Turnberry, which has a four-star hotel almost on the seashore, was the venue for the European Open in September 1979.

I must admit that I used to think my fellow Scots were a bit mad spending so much time trying to hit a wee white ball out of sight. But a few years ago we moved to a house beside the golf course at Kilmacolm.

Now, it is a case of 'if you can't beat 'em, join 'em', so I have started taking lessons. You will not see my name featuring in the British Open, but I am beginning to understand the attraction of the game, and today when I walk my dog over the golf course, I take a five-iron along as well.

If you like walking as much as I do, then I suggest you come to Ayrshire, where there is sea and sand for the children, and places full of interest for adults. The ruined castle at Dunure, which is one of the prettiest fishing villages on the whole coastline, used to belong to the powerful

Culzean Castle, Strathclyde, built round an ancient tower of the Kennedy family but dating mainly from 1777, when Robert Adam remodelled it.

Kennedy family. They were the Kings of Carrick and they had castles everywhere.

The Kennedys were a fearsome clan. In days gone by when someone refused to give up his land, the fourth Earl of Kennedy had him stripped and roasted at Dunure until the poor man agreed to sign away his birthright.

I always think of this grim tale when I am wandering about the ruins of Dunure Castle. On

the other hand, Greenan Castle, near my parents' home at Doonfoot, has no such associations that I know of, and I often walk my dog there.

One castle on this coastline which has survived the ravages of time is Culzean Castle. It was another Kennedy stronghold and its fortifications, together with its position high above Culzean Bay, made it well nigh impregnable. It was remodelled by Robert Adam in the eighteenth century and was given to the National Trust for Scotland in 1945 by the Marquis of Ailsa.

Today Culzean is one of the National Trust showpieces, a truly magnificent castle. I am not surprised that ex-President Eisenhower was so delighted when he was given one of the private flats there as a tribute to his achievement as Supreme Commander of the Allied Forces in World War II.

There are still Kennedys in Ayrshire. The chief of the Kennedy clan is the Marquis of Ailsa, who owns Maybole Castle and Cassillis House, which stands high above the river Doon.

And that brings me back full circle to my favourite spot in Ayrshire, the romantic 'banks and braes o' bonnie Doon'.

THE ROAD TO THE ISLES

A far croonin' is pullin' me away
As I take wi' my cromak to the road...

'The Road to the Isles' is the haunting song of a siren beckoning you to follow her. Listen to the magical lure in the lines 'A far croonin' is pullin' me away' and 'The far Coolins are puttin' love on me...' The writer is being drawn away by some irresistible force.

Yet he cannot keep up for long the pretence that he is going there against his will. There is joy in every word as he talks of the sunlight on his back, the cromak (stick) in his hand and the heather tracks which have scent of heaven about them. The very thought of the islands, he maintains, would put a 'leap among the lame' (make the lame bound with energy to get there).

In the refrain, tracing the road he will take, the writer defends his exuberance by explaining that if you cannot understand it, then you have never smelt the 'tangle' of the Isles.

The lyrics of the song were written by Kenneth MacLeod, who lived on Gigha; the melody was taken from the chanter-playing of Malcolm Johnson and was arranged by Patuffa Kennedy Fraser. Between them all they have produced a song which transcends parochial boundaries and appeals to anyone who is far away from a favourite spot and longing to be back there.

Yet there is no cloying sentimentality about the lyric. I love singing it because the music is so lively and the words are so stirring that I want to put on my walking shoes and start out immediately for the Western Isles. And thereby hangs a question: where exactly *is* the Road to the Isles?

I am not surprised that so many different answers have been given; after all, your route will depend entirely on where you start from. However, if you follow the words of the song, then you will take your cromak (and probably your car) and head for the heartland of Scotland. Pitlochry in Perthshire would seem to be a good starting-point, since it lies in the wooded valley of the river Tummel, and the song, after all, urges you to go by Tummel and Loch Rannoch.

Once you arrive in Pitlochry, you might be tempted to linger a while before proceeding on that celebrated road. Everywhere there are woods, rivers and mountains to delight the eye.

My first visit to Pitlochry was with the Kirkintilloch Junior Choir when we were asked to sing at the Pitlochry Theatre Festival. This 'theatre in the hills' has a summer season of drama, concerts and other entertainment.

Like most youngsters, we were fascinated by dams, and since Pitlochry is an important part of the Hydro Electrical Board's Tummel valley scheme, the dams were spectacular. The Clunie Dam, built at the outlet of the river Tummel, enables 2,700 million gallons of water per day to feed the Pitlochry power station. When another dam was built at the lower end of the Tummel in 1951, a new beauty spot was created: Loch Faskally. When you see boats cruising on this tranquil sheet of water, it is hard to believe that man and not nature was responsible for all this.

At the southern end of the loch is Pitlochry's celebrated fish ladder. I have seen other fish ladders in Scotland, but none as elaborate as the one at Pitlochry. There are thirty-four pools connected by underwater pipes and a 1,000-foot-long observation chamber.

I could stand and stare for hours at the salmon leaping up the ladders while I wonder about the strange instincts which make them return to their birthplace to spawn.

Downstream from the high-level bridge which carries the Road to the Isles across the river Garry, you can walk through woods of oak, spruce and sycamore to the Linn (pool) of Tummel where the water once cascaded down in a mighty waterfall. The hydro-electric schemes reduced the flow but not the natural beauty of the surroundings, which have been taken over by the National Trust. The Trust provides guides to the fauna and flora on the nature trail that runs through the area. From the Linn, there are

At the top of the Sma' Glen, striking out for the Western Isles.

several walks which take you back to Pitlochry.

The town is overlooked by dappled Ben Vrackie (2,757 feet) and if you are athletic enough to climb it, you can make the descent to the Pass of Killiecrankie, a wooded gorge through which the river Garry flows to join the Tummel.

In 1689 Graham of Claverhouse, Viscount Dundee, led his Jacobite followers through this famous pass and annihilated the troops of King William who were positioned at the other end. The Highlanders must have been a fearsome sight since they took off their plaids and socks for the attack, and Clan Chief Lochiel even threw away his shoes so that he could charge barefoot with his men. Perhaps the government troops took one look at the half-clad Highlanders and fled for their lives.

The narrowest part of the gorge is a place known as the Soldier's Leap, where a government soldier is reputed to have jumped eighteen feet across the river to escape the angry Highlanders behind him. Visitors stand there measuring the distance with their eyes, obviously wondering if they would have had the courage to do the same. Had it been me, I think I would just have surrendered.

Claverhouse, Viscount Dundee, was the hero of the Killiecrankie victory. Though he died in the battle, at least he is commemorated in a song — a favourite of mine called 'Bonnie Dundee'.

To the Lords of convention 'twas Claverhouse
      spoke,
Ere the King's crown go down there are crowns to
      be broke,
So let each cavalier who loves honour and me,
Come follow the bonnets of Bonnie Dundee.

Come fill up my cup, come fill up my can,
Come saddle your horses and call up your men,
Come open the west port and let me gang free,
For it's up wi' the bonnets of Bonnie Dundee.

Whenever I sing this song I cannot help visualizing those wild Highlanders throwing off their socks and plaids and charging into the pass howling like banshees.

In the wooded valley of the Tummel, there are wonderful views everywhere you look, but the best one is from a projecting spur at the foot of the loch, where the splendid panorama of mountains, woods and rivers is called the Queen's View. The queen concerned was Queen Victoria, who came here during her tour of the Highlands in 1844. Since she looked down on Loch Tummel from that rocky spur towards the peak of Schiehallion, the 'fairy hill of the Caledonians', there have been many other visitors.

Although Schiehallion is 3,547 feet high, it is an easy climb to the top, and the view of the scenery from the summit is magnificent: Perthshire's peaks and glens lie before you in endless vistas of colour, changing with the seasons.

Loch Rannoch, flanked by the Black Wood of Rannoch.

I feel that it is best to take the Road to the Isles in the spring, because at that time of year the colours are as vibrant and cheerful as the song itself. The woods are carpeted with a blue haze of anemones, creamy blackthorn is spilling over the hedgerows, and when you see the buds bursting on the trees and flowers you cannot help rejoicing at this resurgence of new life.

The road which runs alongside Loch Tummel's seven-mile length takes you to Tummel Bridge. From there you can go to Fortingall, Aberfeldy and Kenmore, But that is not the road to follow if you are heading for the Isles. The route in the song is 'by Tummel and Loch Rannoch and Lochaber'.

You reach Loch Rannoch by driving along the high road to Kinlochrannoch, a small village at the loch's eastern end. Kinlochrannoch has long been renowned as a fisherman's paradise because of the plump trout and salmon which lurk in the pools of the adjoining river Tummel.

Loch Rannoch is nine-and-a-half miles long, a little bigger than Loch Tummel, and there are roads running along both the north and south shores. The road along the southern shore runs past the high steep hills and the Black Wood of

Rannoch, where some of the Scots pines, relics of the primeval Caledonian forest, are seventy feet high and fourteen feet wide, and are judged to be over 250 years old. However, most people claim that the northern road is the Road to the Isles. At one time there was no road there, since it ended at Rannoch station. Beyond is the lonely splendour of Rannoch Moor, surely the most awesome moor in Scotland. Once a wilderness covered with ice, then with firs, the trees were cut down to get rid of the wolves and since then the area has been a vast expanse of moss, boulders, peat and lochs. The peat is twenty foot thick in places and walkers are warned not to stray from well established paths because of the patches of sinking bog. When the engineers were constructing a railway across the moor, they overcame the problem of putting in foundations by building in sticks and heather which would become impregnated with peaty water and would not rot.

In gloomy weather, Rannoch Moor is a chilling place, but when the sun pierces the clouds and illuminates the landscape, it can take on a different aura. One of my friends has a picture hanging above her fireplace of Rannoch Moor bathed in early morning sunlight. The sky is blue, the birches lean gracefully over a small loch and the muted greens and blues of the distant mountains make Rannoch Moor seem a haven of peace.

None the less, I would not like to be alone on Rannoch Moor on a dark afternoon in winter. Glencoe to the west stirs the same ambivalent feelings in me. If you drive along the road from Rannoch Moor to Loch Leven on a day when the sun is shining, it is a positive pleasure to arrive at Glencoe. Lights reflected on the silken waters of the lochans, the wild grandeur of the surrounding hills, and the peaceful green countryside all combine to convince you that this is the most magnificent glen in Scotland.

Unfortunately Glencoe did not achieve fame because of its beauty but because of the bloodbath which took place there on 13 February 1692. The clan Macdonald, who ruled over this part of the country or had done so in past years, had been extending Highland hospitality for twelve days to Captain Campbell of Glenlyon and his soldiers. Some of the Macdonalds were uneasy but their chief MacIan felt he had no cause for alarm. Although he had been the last of the clan chiefs to submit his oath of allegiance to William III and although he had been six days late in handing over his oath at Inveraray, he had complied with the King's command.

Chief MacIan did not know that the enemies of the clan had not forwarded an explanation for his delay — the snow and bad weather — to the King's advisers, and that the King had therefore ordered the extirpation of the clan Macdonald. Lulled into a false sense of security, the chief's son played cards with the commander of the soldiers, but early next morning the soldiers attacked and massacred men, women and children alike. Forty Macdonalds were killed and many of the others who fled died in the hills, and from that day onwards the Macdonalds and the Campbells were locked in hate-filled rivalry. It is all past history now, of course, but if the clouds blot out the sun when you are standing in the Pass of Glencoe, history's ghosts seem to crowd in on you.

Glencoe and Dalness are so beautiful that they were the first stretches of mountainous country to be bought by the National Trust. It is a vast area: 12,000 acres of rugged mountain country approximately forming a triangle, each side of which measures about six miles long, between the rivers Etive and Coe and the Aonach Eagach ridge. In this area is the mountain of Bidean nam Bian, the highest summit in Argyll, flanked by its 'Three Sisters'. Other mountains encompassed by this region include the steep and jagged Aonach Etive Mor. Stob Dearg, the northeastern peak of the latter, looms imperiously above Rannoch Moor to the east.

The Road to the Isles still beckons: 'By Tummel and Loch Rannoch and Lochaber I will go...' Lochaber is another vast area, bounded by Glen Spean and Loch Lochy to the west and by Loch Linnhe and Loch Leven to the east. To the north of Loch Leven lies Fort William.

Fort William was once an earth-and-wattle fort, built by General Monk in 1655. It was rebuilt in stone, attacked, defended and finally demolished in the nineteenth century. The opening of a railway created a new town and today Fort William is a popular holiday centre.

I have been there many times, both as a holiday-maker and as a singer. I enjoy browsing through the West Highland Museum in the High Street, where the exhibits include tartans and Jacobite relics, including the bed where Bonnie

Loch Linnhe, one of the lochs linked together by the Caledonian Canal.

Prince Charlie slept. There is also a secret portrait which you can see only if you reflect it on to the curved surface of a polished cylinder.

If you cannot see much of Ben Nevis, Britain's highest mountain, from Fort William, you have a perfect view of it from Inverlochy Castle, now converted into an elegant and luxurious hotel.

By the time the traveller on the Road to the Isles has reached Fort William, the 'blue islands' will be beckoning him westwards along the northern shores of Loch Eil to the head of Loch Shiel and Glenfinnan.

On a spring day when the sun is shining, the waters of Loch Shiel reflect the changing moods of the mountains, deepening in tone and texture as the day lengthens. Overlooking the loch is a tower topped by the statue of a kilted Highlander. The Glenfinnan monument is a poignant reminder of that day in August 1745 when Bonnie Prince Charlie unfurled his father's standard and launched his attempt to restore the Stuarts to the throne.

The Prince had landed from France on the coast twelve miles to the west. With him were seven faithful followers. It seems incredible to me that he came with only seven men, but the Prince fervently believed that the clans would rally to his cause. Once he had the support of the Macdonalds and of the powerful Cameron of Lochiel, he felt victory was attainable.

Eigg and Rhum, from Arisaig.

When Queen Victoria visited the monument, in September 1873, she wrote in her Highland Journal:

As we suddenly came upon Loch Shiel from a narrow glen lit up by bright sunshine with the fine long loch and rugged mountains which are about 3,000 feet high rising all around... I thought I never saw a lovelier or more romantic spot or one which told its history so well. What a scene it must have been in 1745. And there was I, the descendant of the Stewarts and of the very King whom Prince Charlie fought to overthrow, sitting and walking about quite privately and peaceably.

When I look at the Glenfinnan monument, I remember not only Bonnie Prince Charlie but also Queen Victoria, standing there in her silks and satins contemplating the tide of history.

And so the song continues: 'It's by Shiel water the track is to the west.'

Loch Shiel runs south-west from Glenfinnan towards Kinlochmoidart, the place where Bonnie Prince Charlie waited with his seven followers. At Moidart there is a row of beech trees known as the seven men of Moidart, a tribute to the Prince's courage in landing with such a small force. The bridle path to Kinlochmoidart used to be a famous 'coffin road' for Highland burials.

Kinlochmoidart is to the south, but the Road to the Isles does not lie to the south; it runs westwards along the hilly shores of Loch Eilt, a

freshwater loch studded with islets. Then at last you come to the sea. Loch Ailort is fringed with saffron weed, seagulls wheel above it and a fresh tangy breeze blows in from the sea. Beyond Lochailort is Loch nan Uamh (the loch of the cave). It was here that Bonnie Prince Charlie landed with such hopes in July 1745 and it was from this same loch that he left for France in September 1746, his dreams shattered.

From here, the song takes you north to Arisaig. Every twist in the road reveals a new scene: high mountains, secluded coves, tiny islets and rocks on which seals lie basking in the sun.

Suddenly, you come upon Morar shore, and your eyes are dazzled by the whiteness of the sands and the sapphire blue of the sea. My favourite Caribbean island is Antigua, and to me the sands at Morar have the same silky feel, though regretfully I admit that the water is not so warm. Perhaps I should be completely honest. . .It is absolutely freezing!

The local people tell me that sometimes you can hear the Morar sands sing. One suggested explanation is that the singing sound is produced by wind blowing on the weathered quartzite of which the sands are made. Its effect is pure magic.

Magical too are the views of the Inner

The Caledonian Canal at Clachnaharry, where it enters the Beauly Firth.

Hebrides, Rhum, Eigg and Muck. I remember a boy at school who could recite the names of the Hebridean islands the way the rest of us recited the ten times table. Since the islands all have strange names, he would chant them like a spell.

'The blue islands from the Skerries to the Lews wi' heather honey taste upon each name...' North of Morar is Mallaig, and this is where the 'terra firma' of the Road to the Isles ends. To reach the islands themselves, you must go by boat. Many people do, and Mallaig has become a bustling little port with ferries and steamers crossing to Skye and the Inner Hebrides.

Morar is the holiday base for many of Mallaig's visitors. Not only does Morar have beautiful sands, it has a quaint little village, famous falls and an adjoining loch which is the deepest inland water in Great Britain: 180 fathoms deep. There is reputed to be a monster in the loch which surfaces whenever a member of the clan Macdonald is about to die. Since I am a Macdonald by marriage, I never watch that loch too closely.

The Loch Morar monster is not, of course, as famous as the one in Loch Ness. I mentioned earlier that your Road to the Isles really depends on your point of departure, so if you do not want to follow the route mapped out for you by the song-writer you can begin your journey at Inverness at the northern end of Loch Ness. The Caledonian Canal runs in a diagonal line from Inverness in the north-east of Scotland to Fort William in the south-west, thereby connecting the North Sea with the Atlantic Ocean. The canal's sixty-mile length is made up of twenty-two miles of canal and thirty-eight miles of waterway linking a series of lochs.

Thomas Telford, the 'Colossus of Roads', was the mastermind behind this fantastic piece of engineering, which cleaves Scotland in two. He overcame construction problems by building twenty-eight locks, the best-known of which, in the south near Banavie, are called Neptune's Staircase.

Since the Caledonian Canal runs through the Great Glen of Scotland, the traveller who follows its course is afforded unrivalled views of some of the most magnificent scenery in Scotland. One day I mean to sail down the canal in one of the steamers which are so popular with summer visitors, because so far I have always travelled by car on this particular Road to the Isles.

In fact, I feel much safer in a car when I am on the road that runs beside Loch Ness. Not that I believe in the monster... Or do I? When you hear that a Vickers research submarine picked up a sonar trace in 520 feet of water near the walls of Urquhart Castle, it does make you wonder.

My favourite Loch Ness monster story is the one about the Italian Airforce pilot who, during the Second World War, said after flying over Loch Ness that he had not only seen the monster, he had sunk it.

I mentioned that monks were among the local people who had reported sightings. The monks probably came from Fort Augustus, where there is a Benedictine monastery. South of Fort Augustus is Invergarry, more than halfway down the Caledonian Canal. At Invergarry, if you branch off along the A87 to the north-west, you will find yourself on another well-known Road to the Isles. There is a wild splendour about the scenery here which stirs your blood and makes you proud to be a Scot.

You rarely see anyone walking in the woods or on the shores of Loch Garry, but somehow the loneliness of this part of Scotland only serves to emphasize the beauties of nature: fine birch trees, fragrant wild flowers and a loch which ripples with the movement of birds and fish.

Glen Garry used to be the stronghold of the Macdonalds, but after the Highland Clearances their crofts were deserted. Many of them are said to have gone to Canada, and there are now 20,000 Macdonalds in Glengarry, Ontario.

Loch Garry is only one of several lochs on this route. After passing Loch Loyne and Loch Cluanie you will find yourself in Glen Shiel, which will lead you to Loch Duich. Somehow you expect to see a castle there, and you will not be disappointed. Eilean Donan is on a rocky promontory and is actually at the meeting-point of three lochs: Loch Long, Loch Duich and Loch Alsh. It sits there on an islet looking more like a painting than reality. The burnished browns and blues of the mountains provide its idyllic setting.

When you leave the castle, the road takes you to Kyle of Lochalsh, from which the isle of Skye is only a five-minute trip across the water.

With your arrival on Skye, the siren has accomplished her task and you will have made a remarkable journey, for the Road to the Isles is nothing less than a pilgrimage of the emotions.

WESTERING HOME

And it's westering home, and a song in the air,
Light in the eye, and it's goodbye to care...

Islands have a special fascination for many of us and in Scotland we are indeed fortunate in the number and variety which are situated both off our west coast and in the north-east, where the Orkneys and Shetlands lie. There are large islands, small islands, bleak islands – and islands which are so soft and balmy that, on a sunny day, you can almost imagine you are somewhere in the Caribbean. But the joy of it is that most of them are within easy reach of our big cities. It is little wonder that during the holiday season people from all over Britain descend on Scotland's coasts.

Yet the appeal of these islands goes far beyond national boundaries. I have met people from all over the world who have either asked me about a particular island or have told me of their personal associations with it. I sometimes think that people abroad know more about Skye, for example, than many native Scots.

The lyrics of the song 'Westering Home' are an expression of love for the writer's own favourite island, Islay, but when I am singing this song I think too of the other Scottish islands, for 'Westering Home' is a song which encapsulates island magic. Islay itself, off the west coast, can be reached from Jura, or from the mainland, sailing from Kennacraig, a terminal for island ferries in the north of Kintyre. The quickest way of all, of course, is by air, and on one occasion when friends mentioned that they wanted to spend a day exploring the island, my husband decided to fly us all there himself.

Our friends knew they would not be able to see the whole of Islay in a day since it is one of the biggest west-coast islands, but they were quite happy to rent a car and see as much as they could. We were surprised, in fact, by the amount of ground we were able to cover.

Much of Islay is green and fertile and, of course, the production of whisky is all-important, with no fewer than eight distilleries on the island.

There are two main types of whisky: grain and malt. Grain whisky is made from malted barley together with unmalted barley and maize, and is distilled in a patent still. Malt whisky, the classic spirit, is made entirely from malted barley and is distilled in a pot still. (Most commercial whiskies are in fact blends.) Some whisky-drinkers maintain that it is the smoke of the burning peat, over which the malt is dried, that gives Scotch whisky its distinctive flavour; others say that the pure burn water with which the sugar is extracted from the ground malt is the important ingredient. The only point on which they all agree is that Scotch whisky is unique.

The word 'whisky' derives from the Scottish Gaelic *uisge beatha,* or water of life, and the Highlanders are known to have been distilling it in the fifteenth century. It was in the eighteenth century, however, that whisky distilling had its most dramatic moments. After the Union of the Parliaments of England and Scotland, the English revenue men came north to hunt out the Scots who were evading tax by distilling whisky illegally. It is said that in Edinburgh alone only eight out of the 408 stills were licensed.

Naturally this led to trouble and there are great tales of Highlanders concealing their whisky from the revenue men, and fighting them for possession when their secret hoards were discovered. I used to love reading stories about these illicit stills, of which, I believe, there are still quite a few.

There may even be a few on Islay, though we never came across anyone who admitted to owning one. The cottage craft of whisky production has grown into a world-famous industry. Although I am not a whisky-drinker, the names of Islay's whisky certainly sound musical to me: Ardbeg, Bowmore, Bruichladdich, Bunnahabhain, Caol Ila, Lagavulin, Laphroaig and Port Ellen. We visited some of these and were delighted to see how well the white distilleries blended into the landscape.

One of the isles of St Kilda, in the western Outer Hebrides. This one is now a nature reserve.

One of the intriguing things about Islay is the way this landscape varies. The east coast is picturesque with its tall cliffs, sandy bays and little coves; the western half of the island has flat green farmlands; and in the south-west at Oa, the headlands and hilly terrain have a lonely, desolate atmosphere.

A moment of peace during a whistle-stop tour of the islands.

Everywhere on Islay there are relics of the past, among them standing stones, fine Celtic crosses and ancient chapels. In his book *Argyll and Bute,* the author Nigel Tranter says that he found more ancient chapels on Islay than in any comparable area he knows. I am sure the chapel members must have been enthusiastic singers because the island has a rich heritage of music. It also has its own special song, 'In Praise of Islay'.

There are so many beautiful islands off the west coast of Scotland that it is difficult to make a choice about which to see, but if you are already on Islay then the obvious thing to do is to take the ferry from Port Askaig on the north coast to the neighbouring island of Jura. On Jura, as on Islay, whisky is an important product, but there is only one distillery, at Craighouse — where most people on the island live.

Jura has two distinctive features, the mountains which bear the appropriate name of 'Paps of Jura' (one of which rises to 2,500 feet) and the whirlpool of Corryvreckan. Long before I ever visited Jura, I had heard of Corryvreckan. There is a legend about the whirlpool, but its reputed danger is certainly no myth. Once a boat has been dragged to its centre, the whirlpool will suck it down to the bottom of the sea.

If you fly back from Jura or Islay as we did, you can catch a glimpse of another island that is worth visiting, Gigha (or 'God's Island', as it is often called). A ferry from Tayinloan on Kintyre will take you to this tiny Inner Hebridean island, only six miles long and one-and-a-half miles wide. It has its own school, a church, a number of cottages and an excellent hotel, but Gigha is worth visiting if only to see the fifty acres of garden created by James Horlick in the Achamore estate. In May and June the azaleas here are a blaze of colour, and so, at other times, are the hydrangeas, fuchsias and magnolias.

Once you are back on the mainland of Kintyre again, you can take the road which runs north from Lochgilphead to Oban, the gateway to the Highlands and an embarkation point for steamers to the islands of Mull, Iona, Staffa, Lismore, Colonsay, Coll, Tiree, Barra and South Uist.

When we have visitors from abroad who have not time to go out to any of the islands, we take them down to Ardrishaig, south of Lochgilphead at the entrance to the Crinan Canal. The canal connects Loch Fyne with the Atlantic Ocean and is a great favourite with yachtsmen. You can spend happy hours here watching gaily coloured yachts and fishing boats negotiating the canal's fifteen locks.

That redoubtable traveller Queen Victoria went along the Crinan Canal by barge in 1847. I can just picture her on deck exclaiming over the beauty of the wooded countryside through which the canal passes, and I can imagine how delighted she would have been when her barge came to the Sound where the canal meets the sea at Crinan. Here, a splendid view unfolds over the rocky islands.

From Crinan, taking the main road north again, you go up past Kilmartin to Kintraw, at the head of the enchanting inlet of Loch Craignish.

Oban, Strathclyde, the starting-point for many a trip to Iona, Staffa and the Outer Hebrides.

North of Loch Craignish is Loch Melfort and from here you see the islands of Luing and Seil. You lose sight of the islands as the road sweeps inland but at Kilninver you can make a detour down to see them. Seil is not really an island at all since it is connected to the mainland by the Clachan Bridge, 'the bridge over the Atlantic'.

I like the whitewashed cottages of Seil and always enjoy going on the ferry to the nearby islands of Easdale and Luing. One of my friends was tempted to buy a house on Luing, but did not like the idea that she might be cut off from the mainland by stormy weather. And this can happen. Although the crossing is very short, the waves can be too rough for the sea crossing. One day when my friend was still debating whether to buy the Luing cottage, she arrived at the ferry to ask if the boatman was crossing. He glanced at the water, ruffled by the sharp breeze, and said, 'Aye, maybe, but then, maybe not.'

I explained to my friend when she was telling me about it that if ever you decide to buy a house on an island that you have to get into the island way of thinking. I still laugh when I think of the notice I once saw outside an island newsagent's shop: 'Sunday papers tomorrow — perhaps!'

Possibly I am a little more in tune with the Highlands and islands than many people because we have so many friends and relations who live there. Although my own childhood memories are bound up with Brora on the northeast coast of Scotland, my husband Stuart spent part of his childhood in the west. His mother came from Taynuilt in Argyll and when the Second World War broke out, she decided to move from Glasgow back to Taynuilt. After all, that was where Aunt Flora and Uncle Dougie, the local farmer, joiner, undertaker and general handyman, lived. Stuart loved it so much that he hated the thought of going back to school. He used to measure the time left to him in haircuts ('Oh no! Two more and I'll have to go back to school').

Naturally Stuart was keen to show me his childhood haunts and we have been back up to Taynuilt many times since our marriage. Once, on one of our flights from Connel, we buzzed Rose Cottage. Aunt Flora and Uncle Dougie came out frantically waving the biggest handkerchiefs they could find.

When visiting Taynuilt we often go on to Oban, which is only ten miles away. Stuart has relatives there too, including an uncle who plays the organ in Christ Church, Dunollie, and I recently sang with the choir there.

Oban is one of the most popular holiday resorts in Scotland. Only a narrow strip of water separates it from the island of Kerrera, and Oban Bay is therefore almost handlocked. The shelter afforded by the bay attracts yachts, ferries and holiday-makers by the thousand. Diversions include the yachting week in August, the Argyllshire Gathering, splendid sands for sunbathing and swimming at Ganavan, an eighteen-hole golf course and two ruined castles, one at Dunollie and the other at Dunstaffnage off the Connel road.

If you want a good view of Oban, it is best to climb the hill behind it. There you will see Mc-Caig's Tower, which looks as if someone started to build a second Coliseum, like the one in Rome, and then changed his mind. In fact, that is not far from the truth. It was a banker who conceived the idea of the building. He intended it to be a museum which he could fill with family relics, but unfortunately he died before the building was completed. I feel it is rather hard on the man to call it McCaig's Folly — its alternative name — because although McCaig was going to make it a family museum, his prime intention was to relieve local unemployment.

Like many other visitors to the area, we have often used Oban as a base for exploring some of the western isles. The steamer sailings from Oban are part of its attraction and I will certainly never forget one memorable occasion when I took the steamer for Mull. I had been invited there to attend the Tobermory Highland Games as a guest and to sing at the ceilidh afterwards. Let me warn all those who have never been at a ceilidh, the Highland word for 'party', that you must (like the Boy Scouts) be prepared for anything. That particular ceilidh started off as a formal concert but it soon became an event in which the audience participation was carried to its full extent.

Tobermory, the Isle of Mull's largest resort and a bustling fishing port.

Everyone joined in the singing, the shouting and the dancing, and that was the beginning of a long night. Bobby MacLeod, who was Provost of Tobermory at that time, was there with his famous dance band and at four in the morning he was playing his pipes along the quayside.

The ceilidh, of course, was well patronized by Gaelic singers, and I was definitely the 'English veesitor'. I must say I felt slightly annoyed at this but when you attend ceilidhs you come to expect it. There is a special atmosphere of camaraderie amongst the Gaels. One of the Gaelic singers at the ceilidh was a man called Kenny Macrae, who just missed his boat back to Oban the following morning. When the Captain heard the identity of the man left on the quayside, he shouted to his crew: 'Och, it's Kenny, is it? Take the boat back!'

I stayed behind to explore Mull. I did not climb its highest peak, Ben More (not after that ceilidh!), but I visited Duart Castle, the ancestral home of the Macleans, travelled through the dramatic pass of Glen More and saw some of the wild scenery near Salen.

I made a special point of seeing Dervaig, home of Mull's Little Theatre. The theatre is manned by Barrie and Marianne Hesketh and must be one of the smallest theatres in the world, seating only forty people. Another fascinating thing I discovered while I was there concerned the Spanish treasure ship which lies at the foot of Tobermory Bay. It seems that it will only be a matter of time before the treasure is recovered and put on public display. The Duke of Argyll is as convinced as the other locals that it exists, and he has pledged the treasure-seekers his support.

When I was in Mull I went across to Iona for the day. Only three-quarters of a mile separates Mull from Iona, a tiny, windswept island covered in wild flowers. St Columba and his monks landed here in AD 563 and became the founders of Christianity in Scotland. The faith they established has certainly survived the 'wrecks of time', as the Scots psalm has it.

To the north of Iona is the island of Staffa. No one lives on Staffa, but it has become famous for its caves — especially Fingal's cave, which inspired Mendelssohn to write his overture *The Hebrides*. This marvellous music paints a vivid picture of the waves crashing into this enormous cave (an amazing 227 feet long and 66 feet high).

As well as sailing to Mull and Iona, I have flown over Colonsay, Oronsay and the Hebridean islands of Coll and Tiree, again with my husband as pilot.

Among the other islands are Barra and Eriskay in the Outer Hebrides. Barra became famous when it was featured in the film of Sir Compton Mackenzie's book *Whisky Galore*. This showed the ingenuity and native cunning of the islanders when faced with a wreck containing a cargo of whisky. They were as anxious to hold on to that whisky as their ancestors were to keep their illicit stills, so the whisky from the wrecked ship was hidden in all sorts of unlikely places such as hot water bottles, vacuum flasks, bread bins and blanket boxes.

Compton Mackenzie's book was founded on fact. In 1941 the *SS Politician* bound for New York was wrecked in the Western Isles and 20,000 bottles of whisky were left floating in the sea. The incident was used to full comic effect.

The *SS Politician* is supposed to have foundered on Eriskay, an island between Barra and South Uist. Eriskay, a tiny, rather barren little island only three miles long by one-and-a-half miles wide, will always have a special place in Scottish history. It was here Bonnie Prince Charlie landed in 1745 when he hoped to win back the Scottish crown for the Stuarts.

Eriskay will be remembered too for its history of Gaelic music. It was Mary MacInnes of Eriskay who first sang the 'Eriskay Love Lilt', a love song which is so sad and beautiful that it has brought tears to my eyes when I have been singing it.

Vair me o ro van o,
    Vair me o ro van eee,
Vair me or ru o ho,
    Sad am I without thee.

When I'm lonely dear white heart
    Black the night or wild the sea,
By love's light my foot finds
    The old pathway to thee.

Thou'rt the music of my heart,
    Harp of joy, oh cruit mo cridh,
Moon of guidance by night,
    Strength and light thou'rt to me.

It does not seem to matter that the words of the refrain ('Vair me o ro van o') are quite meaningless: the plaintive melody stirs your soul.

Some of the songs of the Western Isles are similar to the *fados*, the melancholy folk-songs of

Portugal. The Portuguese say the *fados* have 'saudade', a sweet sadness, and this is certainly true of the 'Eriskay Love Lilt'. 'Westering Home', on the other hand, brims over with laughter and liveliness. The contrast in the words, music and style of the two songs is as vivid as the contrast between the islands themselves.

However, there is one island in Scotland which seems to combine features of all the others and of the mainland too. Perhaps that is why the isle of Arran is called 'Scotland in miniature'. There are towering mountains which look as if they have been plucked from a range in the Highlands, stretches of sloping pastures which could have come from the Lowlands, picturesque villages, beautiful golden sands and rivers which, though a tenth of the size of the Tay in Perthshire, are still temptingly full of salmon and sea trout. There are caves, castles and facilities for almost every hobby and sport imaginable.

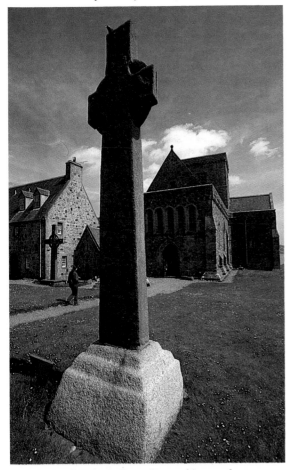

The sixteen-foot-high Great Cross of Iona at Iona Abbey, Inner Hebrides.

Needless to say, there are golf courses, too. (Nowhere could be called 'Scotland in miniature' without one.) In fact there are seven golf courses, for Arran is bigger than many of the other west-coast islands (twenty miles from north to south and nine miles wide).

One of the island's other great advantages is its accessibility. It lies in the Firth of Clyde and the steamer leaves from Ardrossan, only an hour's drive from Glasgow. Once you are on the boat, it takes an hour to reach Brodick, the village which considers itself to be the island's capital.

A two-hour journey from Glasgow may seem quite long, but many people come every year to Arran from as far away as south-west England, Wales and Ireland. You hear foreign tongues, too, as you sit on the Arran buses. Yet the strange thing about Arran is that although people disembark from each ferry in their hundreds, the island absorbs them all, and the visitor's most lasting impression of Arran will be of its peace: long stretches of empty road, moorland and mountain with not a soul in sight, and green glens which are covered with wild hyacinths and bluebells in the spring and in the summer glow with fuchsia, honeysuckle and foxglove.

The island is also unusual in that you can drive right round it, and in that it has only one inland village, Shiskine. Holiday-makers agree to disagree about which part of the island is the best. I have some friends who prefer Brodick because it has the best anchorage for yachts, the highest peak on the island (Goatfell, 2,866 feet) and Brodick Castle, with its fine rhododendrons.

Others say that Brodick is far too busy, so they much prefer small villages like Corrie, Lochranza or Lamlash, which has the best sporting facilities, and fans of Blackwaterfoot say that its sands and golf course make that the top resort. Certainly few golf courses can boast a hole like the 'Crow's Nest', a platform of green from which you have marvellous views of Arran and the Kintyre coast.

Many miles from Arran and the other western isles are the Orkneys and Shetlands. The Shetlands, in particular, seem when you visit them like the end of the world. They *are* a long way away: sixty miles north of the Orkneys, which makes them the most northerly part of Britain. The islands vary in shape and size but they are all deeply indented with sea lochs (or 'voes', as they are called in Shetland). Sullom Voe is so deep it can accommodate the biggest tankers in the world. When you fly to Shetland – and flying is the easiest way to get there – you have a marvellous view of the islands as the plane comes in to land.

There are over a hundred islands in the archipelago but only seventeen are inhabited. When I was there I felt very conscious of the fact that wherever you are in Shetland, the sea is only a few miles away. The Shetlanders' main industry used to be fishing. Then came the oil boom. Pipelines, marine terminals and oil-related industries were suddenly transforming the economy and the appearance of the islands.

I am full of admiration for the way the people in Shetland have adapted to the bonanza on their back doorstep (the oil was found a hundred miles north-east of the Shetlands) and I am sure some of the oil company bosses must have been surprised by the toughness and tenacity with which the Shetlanders fought to ensure that some of this new wealth would be used to benefit the islands. Perhaps the Shetlanders have inherited some of the sterling qualities of their ancestors, the Vikings, who conquered the Shetland Isles in AD 800 and did not give them up till 1469 when King Christian of Denmark pledged them to James III as his daughter's dowry.

You do not have to look far to see evidence of Shetland's past. If you fly to Sumburgh, which is the airport of Mainland, the principal island in the Shetland group, you can wander round nearby Jarlshof. This is the excavated site of three villages dating, respectively, from the Bronze Age, the Iron Age and the Viking period.

There are ancient remains on the other islands as well. On the island of Mousa, off the east coast of Mainland, stands a famous broch – a high round tower with double walls, galleries and stairs. It was used for defending the Shetlands long before they were captured by the Norsemen. The broch at Mousa is supposed to be the best-preserved example in Scotland. Another one can be seen in the outskirts of Lerwick, the capital of Mainland.

Lerwick is unlike any other place I have been to in Scotland. When I was there, the lively port always seemed to be crowded with Scandinavian and Russian fishermen. The babble of foreign languages made me feel that I was abroad. In Shetland this feeling is intensified by the long

One of the crofts on Shetland's Mainland, nestling in a quiet inlet.

summer nights in which the sun never sets. How marvellous to live in such a place in summer! On the other hand, the winters must seem endless.

Because of this, the islanders make a big event of their 'Up Helly Aa' festival, held at the end of January when winter is on the wane: a real cause for celebration. I have watched this festival many times on television and it is certainly one of the most dramatic in Britain. A torch-lit replica of a Viking longship is borne through the streets and then burned in a ceremony which is reminiscent of a Viking funeral.

Before the oil boom, the main occupation of the Shetland men was fishing, and the women spent their time knitting the dyed wool from the Shetland sheep. These sheep are brown and black, unlike the white sheep of the mainland.

I was fascinated by the sheep, especially when I heard that the wool is not shorn from them but plucked from the animals' necks. The shops were full of Shetland knitwear and naturally we bought some to take home with us. (I adored the Shetland ponies, too, but had to be content with just looking at them.)

Some of the sweaters in the Shetland shops came from Fair Isle, which is famous not just for its knitwear but for its breeding colonies of fulmars, storm petrels and Arctic skuas. Since many migrating birds seem to use Fair Isle as a staging post, it is a mecca for ornithologists.

A farm on Fair Isle, Britain's most remote inhabited island.

Fair Isle lies midway between Shetland and Orkney. It was an invitation to sing that first took me there. The Orkneys are not as remote as the Shetlands, being only seven miles from John o' Groats. There are seventy islands, but only about a third of them are inhabited. I travelled by boat and how well I remember that trip across the Pentland Firth on the *SS St Ola*. The Firth can be very stormy, but I have always been a good sailor and when I get on deck I turn my face to the wind. There is a song which captures that feeling:

Sailing homeward sing we merrily
Ho ro chase the breeze
Through the spume and through the spindrift
Ho ro chase the breeze.

The principal island of Orkney, like that of Shetland, is called Mainland. Approaching it from Shetland, you pass the high cliffs of the island of Hoy with the Old Man of Hoy, a 450-foot pillar of sandstone, standing beside it.

In Kirkwall, the capital of Mainland, I was looking forward to seeing St Magnus Cathedral, an impressive Norman building with a strange history. Magnus Erlendsson was a Norse earl who ruled over the Orkneys with his relative Hakon Paulson. Unfortunately the two men quarrelled and friends had to arrange a peace conference. The two earls promised to attend with a few friends and only two ships. Magnus kept his word, but Hakon brought eight ships and allowed one of his attendants to cleave Magnus' skull with an axe. Magnus was buried in a church in Birsay and very soon there were reports of magical cures occurring. This led to Magnus being canonized and his body was taken to the cathedral founded in his honour by his nephew in 1137. When Magnus's remains were found by workmen in the cathedral, they could still see the axe wound in his skull.

The old town of Kirkwall clusters round the cathedral as if for protection, and it was a delight to walk along flagged streets with no pavements and gaze up at the grey stone houses with their crow-stepped gables.

In Orkney, as in Shetland, there are ancient remains. There is a megalithic burial chamber at Maes Howe, a ruined palace at Birsay, the Stone Circles at Stenness and a farm museum at Corrigall. Stromness is the second biggest town on the island of Mainland and near it is the Stone Age village of Skara Brae with its circular houses.

Historical reminders of more recent times can be seen in Kirkwall's Tankerness House Museum. This is where I saw how the crofters used to live and, coincidentally, fell in love with the tall-backed Orkney chairs made of woven straw.

More than anything else, however, it is the music of these Northern Isles that I remember. Everyone there seems to sing and the skill of the fiddlers is staggering. After a concert in Shetland years ago I was given a copy of an old song which had been handed down from generation to generation. I still have it, and it has that special quality that sets island songs apart. Writers of these lyrics understood island magic: visit one island and another one will beckon.

THE BIRKS OF ABERFELDY

Bony lassie will ye go, will ye go;
Bony lassie will ye go to the birks of Aberfeldy?

Have you ever wondered where you can see the most perfect freshwater pearl in the world? Do you know where the finest salmon-fishing waters in Britain are? Where is the longest river in Scotland? And do you know where Princess Margaret was born? The answer in each case is Tayside, the newly created region which covers the larger part of Perthshire and the old counties of Angus and Kinross.

I like the new name of Tayside because the river Tay runs through the region like a silver thread adding lustre to each place it passes. Tayside itself has many happy memories for me. I have taken part in television spectaculars that have been filmed there, toured the countryside singing at concerts, and once I had the unforgettable experience of being driven through the fair city of Perth in a tartan Rolls-Royce.

Perth has other, more intimate, memories for me, too. My husband-to-be bought my engagement and wedding rings in Perth and it was in Perth that I was allowed to hold the most perfect pearl in the world.

But before I tell you about Perth itself, let me introduce you to Tayside. Since there are two thousand square miles of it, with a population of half a million, it would be impossible to describe it all, so let me tell you about the parts I know. My knowledge of Scottish geography did not begin with books. The regions became familiar to me through the lyrics associated with them.

Aberfeldy is no exception. Long before I went there, I had sung 'The Birks of Aberfeldy' many times. According to a note in the Kilmarnock edition of Robert Burns' works the poet said: 'I composed these stanzas standing under the Falls of Moness near Aberfeldy.'

Yet, curiously enough, there are very few 'birks' (birch trees) at Aberfeldy, which has made some people conclude that the words were written to the air of an older lyric, 'The Birks of

Abergeldie'. But whatever doubts there are about the origin of the song, its popular appeal is not in question.

The song is best sung as a duet, and when a handsome tenor is looking into my eyes and pleading with me to go to the Birks of Aberfeldy with him. I can hardly prevent myself saying, 'Yes, yes, of course I'll go' – a very natural reaction, surely, if he wants to take me to one of my favourite places in Scotland?

It is an easy enough place to reach. If you are touring in Perthshire, inevitably you will find yourself at some stage in the centre of the county at Crieff. From Crieff there is a road through the Sma' Glen which leads on to Amulree and then Aberfeldy. I have been up in that part of the country many times.

Crieff, one of the gateways to the Highlands, is a small town seventeen miles west of Perth, but to Glaswegians and to many other Scots, Crieff is 'The Hydro'. The Hydro has long been a favourite holiday hotel for Scots, partly because of its moderate terms, but also because of the spaciousness of its interior. The long, wide corridors were not designed specifically for childish romps, but there are few children who can resist the temptation to race each other down them or to slide along the polished surfaces on their bottoms. The swimming pool, the tennis court and the frequent dances held there all contribute to the hotel's popularity.

Crieff enjoys a commanding position overlooking the river Earn. The nearby waterfalls at Loch Turret and the beautiful glens that surround the town make Crieff an enchanting place to visit.

My usual reason for visiting the town was to sing at the Ochtertyre theatre. The eighteenth-century mansion of Ochtertyre was owned by the late Sir William Murray, who was so interested in the arts that he made part of Ochtertyre into a theatre and many artists, including myself, were invited to perform there.

Blair Castle, Tayside, built by the Duke of Atholl in a position of strategic importance to the Central Highlands.

Attempting to turn a private house into a theatre was an act of courage, but sadly it was not a commercial success. Today there are no Murrays living in Ochtertyre, but whenever I pass it, I remember the applause of an audience which succeeded in making every performer feel like an honoured guest.

The road from Crieff to Aberfeldy, which was built in 1730 by the soldiers of General Wade, leader of the army against the Highlanders during the Jacobite risings, passes through the Sma' Glen. In point of fact this moorland valley is four miles long, so it is not all that small, but it is undeniably dramatic. The gorge through which the river Almond threads its path is very narrow and the narrowness is accentuated by the steep hills on either side.

When General Wade's soldiers found their passage blocked by a mighty rock called Ossian's Stone, they set about removing it. Underneath, they discovered a prehistoric burial-place. Ossian's Stone now sits at the north end of the pass, a vast, ice-bound boulder which keeps its own secrets.

The Wade road runs north from the Sma' Glen to Amulree, a delightful hamlet ringed by hills which tempt the climber. You can go from Amulree through lonely Glen Quaich to Kenmore on Loch Tay, but the direct route to Aberfeldy takes you on a steeply rising road past little Loch na Craige to the summit of Glen Cochill.

There you can look down on Aberfeldy and the fertile valley of Strathtay, while the lovely peak of Perthshire's fairy mountain, Schiehallion, soars up in the west.

General Wade's road disappears to the west, but in Aberfeldy itself there is a reminder of the famous general in a five-arched bridge over the river Tay. At its south end is a monument of a kilted figure who commemorates the raising of the Black Watch, the regiment which was supposed to keep peace in the Highlands. As a child, I used to think they were called Black Watch because of their black deeds, but I learned later that the name merely reflects the fact that those fine soldiers wore dark tartan to distinguish them from the Redcoats.

Aberfeldy is supposed to have been named after a water-sprite, which seems very appropriate in view of all the water surrounding it.

The little town sits demurely on the banks of the river Tay, some six miles from Loch Tay. As for the Falls of Moness, which inspired Burns' song 'The Birks of Aberfeldy', they are only a short distance away.

To see the Falls properly, you need to go along the path opposite the Breadalbane Arms and then spend at least two hours exploring the area. The Scottish Wildlife Trust have marked out a nature trail which takes you past the lowest fall, about a mile from the starting-point, and leads you to the second and third falls almost a mile further on.

When you reach the rustic bridge and admire the view, you realize that no poet could have found more appropriate words than these:

The braes ascend like lofty wa's,
The foamy stream deep roaring fa's
O'erhung wi' fragrant-spreading shaws,
The birks of Aberfeldy.

...White o'er the linns the burnie pours
And rising, weets wi' misty showers,
The birks of Aberfeldy.

The last time I was up in that part of Tayside, I was filming a joint BBC/Dutch television production. The Dutch wanted Scottish scenes as a background for the Scottish songs I was singing. Some people are inclined to think that television shows are created very quickly but, as I know only too well, this is not the case. Choosing suitable locations for songs takes much time and care; then there are weather problems and all the detailed work involved in moving a film unit and artists from place to place.

Some of the filming for this particular show was done in the region west of Aberfeldy. One of the locations was Kenmore, which proved to be an excellent choice in every way. Nearby is Taymouth Castle, which has been the home of a marquis, a Civil Defence Training Centre and a school for the children of Americans in Scotland. There are now plans to turn it into a youth hostel.

If Taymouth Castle is unusual, so is the village of Kenmore. It was created in the eighteenth century by the third Earl of Breadalbane, a far-sighted man if ever there was one. When he constructed Kenmore, he decreed that the villagers would pay no rent if they kept their cottages and gardens sparkling and colourful. This was not exactly an act of altruism. The earl's main concern

Loch Tay, on the river Tay just below Aberfeldy.

was to ensure that the view from his house was not spoilt for his guests.

The long-term effects of his policy have been beneficial for everyone, because Kenmore came to be known as one of the most attractive villages in Scotland. It was greatly admired by William and Dorothy Wordsworth when they visited it, and Robert Burns was so impressed by the trim, white-painted cottages that he was inspired to write a poem about the view of the village from its bridge spanning the river Tay.

The river Tay is a magnificent stretch of water. The longest river in Scotland, 120 miles in length, it rises on the north slope of Ben Lui in the heart of Perthshire at 3,000 feet, then follows a willowy path through a catchment area of 2,400 square miles before it reaches the north-east coast at Dundee. In fact the river Tay carries the largest volume of water of any British river.

Loch Tay itself is dominated on its northern shore by lofty mountains which reach their highest point in Ben Lawers (only 16 feet short of 4,000 feet). The Loch is fifteen miles long, and its beauty is enhanced by some wooded islands, the largest of which is Eilean nam Ban, the island of women.

It seems strange that an 'island of women' should be in the middle of a loch which is dominated by men. I am referring to the fishermen, of course, who come here because the Tay is one of

the best salmon-fishing waters in Britain. The start of the salmon-fishing season, in January, is a very serious business. A piper in full regalia pipes the anglers to the loch. I would have thought that the noise of the bagpipes would have made any salmon jump ten feet out of the water. If they do so near the shore, the salmon are liable to become inebriated because custom dictates that a bottle of whisky is broken over the bows of the first boat to be launched.

I have never caught a salmon, but I am sure it is only a matter of time before I catch a trout − not in the Tay but in my own garden, where my husband has stocked a large pool with American brook trout. Once I become expert at catching trout, maybe I will venture out on Loch Tay − without bagpipes.

Many people have tried to describe Loch Tay but no one has succeeded as well as Sir Walter Scott, who sang its praises in his novel *The Fair Maid of Perth*.

As the river Tay flows north-east out of Loch Tay, past Kenmore and Aberfeldy, it follows a long, winding course to Perth.

At Meikleour, east of the Great North Road and famed for its enormously tall beech hedge, the Tay is joined by the river Isla, a splendid tributary. The Isla itself has already received, some miles upstream, the waters of two fine rivers, the Ericht and the Dean, and on the latter stands Glamis Castle, birthplace of Princess Margaret. The entrance to the castle lies just off the main road from Coupar Angus to Forfar and it can therefore be easily reached from all points.

Many years ago I was thrilled to take part in a television sequence that was being filmed at the

Left The source of the longest river in Scotland, the Tay. *Above* Frightening away the salmon!

castle, and I have visited it many times since then. I recall one occasion in particular when the rain was pouring down and the castle was wreathed with mist. It seemed a very appropriate setting for Shakespeare's *Macbeth*, whose hero was of course Thane of Glamis. The setting seemed very suitable, too, for the Lady Glamis who was accused of being a witch and burned at the stake in Edinburgh in 1537.

In later and happier years, Glamis was the

home of Lady Elizabeth Bowes-Lyon, now Queen Elizabeth the Queen Mother, and her daughter Princess Margaret Rose was born here, the first royal baby to be born in Scotland in three hundred years.

The castle is open to the public from May until September and there is much to see: a beautiful avenue, a marvellous crypt and gardens designed by Capability Brown. One thing you cannot see is the secret chamber which is supposed to be known only to the Earls of Strathmore and their

The romantic spires of Glamis Castle, ancestral home of the Earl of Strathmore.

heirs when they come of age. Although I did not see the secret chamber, the Earl and Countess of Strathmore showed me the little room where our present Queen and her sister once played. You can still see their names on the door where they used to measure their height: Lilibet and Margaret Rose.

Further along the Tay lies Dunkeld. On shaded lawns beside the river stand the ruins of Dunkeld Cathedral, which dates back to the fourteenth century. It has a wonderful atmosphere

and delightful surroundings. For this, all credit must be given to the National Trust, which decided to restore the 'little houses' in the cathedral precinct and in doing so have managed to preserve their unique character.

At this point the river Tay is an impressive sight, flowing broad and swift between Dunkeld on the north bank and Birnam on the south. This little village was made famous by Shakespeare in *Macbeth*. The three witches prophesied that Macbeth would die when Birnam Wood came to Dunsinane, and when this prophecy appeared to come true he began to realize he was doomed. On the right bank of the Tay, there is a terrace walk amongst the trees of Birnam Wood, but even if I am there in bright sunshine, I am transported back to my schooldays, the dark drama of *Macbeth* and Shakespeare's poetry.

Talking of poetry and Perthshire, I simply have to mention in passing the Rhyming Bard, who lives at Bridge of Cally, north-east of Dunkeld. Although I have never actually met him he has been writing poetry to me ever since I started my professional career and every year on our wedding anniversary he sends us a card. In fact, he claims that writing verses to me started him off on his own career as a poet. Here is part of one of his first poems to us:

I send you congratulations due
To you and handsome husband Stu
The sweetest singer on God's earth
You gave my pen poetic birth.

To prove his point, he sends me every poem he has published in newspapers and magazines. I must admit it is a great ego-booster when one of his poems pops through the letter box.

Dear Lassie wi' the chestnut locks
Bright smiling face and gorgeous looks,
This nicht 'The Muse' I'll try to woo
And send my verse in thanks to you.

After that poem arrived I sat at my kitchen table visualizing some young Scotsman who looked like a cross between Robert Redford and Paul Newman. Then I received the Rhyming Bard's next poem:

I'm getting auld and gey near bauld
My step is slow and short…

Ah well…

I do not care what the Bard o'Ardle Glen (as he calls himself) looks like, I think it is fantastic that he has been writing poetry to me for all these years. Such sentiments as 'You're still by far the brightest star from Wick to hilly Wales' can hardly help but brighten up a bleak Monday morning.

So much for the Rhyming Bard. Meanwhile, the Tay has passed Dunkeld and swept on through peaceful countryside to reach Perth, the Fair City.

Perth, on the west bank of the Tay, owes much of its beauty to the river and the bridges which span it. Adjacent to the river two large open spaces, the North and South Inches, make a splendid setting for the elegant houses which line both banks.

The North Inch was used in the fourteenth century as a combat arena for two opposing clans, Clan Chattan and Clan Kay, who were helped in their struggle by a bandy-legged blacksmith who was brought in at the last moment because the Clan Chattan were a man short. He was the one who is supposed to have survived this epic confrontation by swimming up the river.

St John's Kirk, where in 1559 John Knox preached his famous sermon against idolatry, which launched the Scottish reformation and gave rise to a wave of opposition to all things Catholic, is one of the oldest buildings in Perth. Nearby Scone Palace is among the most magnificent. The home of the Earls of Mansfield, it contains many priceless treasures.

My main reasons for visiting Perth have been to sing at concerts in the town hall and to attend services in St John's Kirk — with one notable exception.

On this occasion, I had been invited to Perth to open a supermarket and someone had decided that it would be an original idea to drive me through the fair city in a Rolls-Royce painted tartan. I was married by that time and my husband was supposed to travel in the car with me, but he took one look at the tartan Rolls-Royce and refused to set foot in it. So while I rode like royalty in the gaudy limousine, Stuart walked behind well out of sight.

Still, Perth has happy memories for my husband too because it was there he bought me my engagement ring some years earlier. A friend told Stuart that if he wanted to buy his fiancée a very special ring, he should go to the Perth jeweller's run by Jimmy and Alastair Cairncross.

While we were looking around the shop, Jimmy Cairncross asked if I would like to see the famous Tay Pearl, whereupon he brought out the most magnificent pearl I have ever seen — half and inch in diameter, 34.5 grains in weight, and said to be the most perfect freshwater pearl in the world. Its perfection lies not in its size but in its quality and lustre. The Cairncross brothers told us that compared with oriental, natural or cult-

Highland calves - not yet old enough to look ferocious!

ured pearls, a perfect freshwater pearl is like a plum on a tree with the bloom still on it. Certainly the pearl in my hand glowed an ethereal pink and lilac. When I jokingly commented that it almost seemed to be alive, Jimmy Cairncross replied gravely that it was a pearl that 'spoke to you'.

Everyone knows it as the Abernethy or the Tay Pearl, but its owners have an affectionate nickname for it, 'little Willie'; and thereby hangs another Perth tale.

In the nineteenth century the Cairncross family opened up a watchmaker's business in Perth. The next generation heard of the pearls being fished out of the river Tay by a local man, William Abernethy, and decided to sell some of them. It was only a small part of their business and it did not begin to expand till 1951 when a descendant of the original Cairncross brothers met up with a descendant of the original pearl fisherman, another William Abernethy, and discovered that he too was fishing the local waters for pearls. It was a coincidence that was to bode well for the future.

Alastair Cairncross had trained in practical jewellery design in London, Jimmy Cairncross was an astute businessman, and they soon realized that Bill Abernethy's pearls would make beautiful centrepieces for brooches, rings and pendants. The colour of the pearls varies from grey, gold, white and pink to lilac, but they all have a lovely, untouched quality about them since they are ready to be set as soon as they are taken out of their shell and need no cutting or polishing. In a word, the pearls which Bill Abernethy fishes from the Tay are unique.

After Perth, at the head of its estuary, the river flows east towards the Firth of Tay, on which stands the city of Dundee. Long famed for jute, jam and journalism, Dundee has passed through very difficult times in recent years. Old industries have sadly declined, but happily fresh opportunities have opened up, some connected with the North Sea oil industry.

But some things have remained the same. Draffens is still the best-known shop in the city and the Caird Hall, bequeathed by Sir James Caird in 1914, is still its most magnificent building, with a fine façade of ten Doric columns.

I remember well my very first appearance

Tayside, location of some of the finest fishing waters in the world.

there, as a singer with the Kirkintilloch Junior Choir. Since the choir's funds were limited, its members were billeted out for an overnight stay. After I had sung my solo at the concert a tall, balding gentleman said that he and his sister would look after the little girl who had sung a song about her grandfather's whiskers. My mother had told me that Draffens was the biggest and best store in Dundee, so I was much impressed when I heard that I was to be taken care of by Sir John Draffen.

The next morning, as a treat, Miss Draffen took me to the store and said that I could choose anything I wanted as a gift. Ali Baba could not

have been more excited when he found the cave of the forty thieves. But, anxious not to seem greedy, I chose a one-shilling diary!

Dundee itself became internationally famous when the first bridge built there across the Tay collapsed as a train was crossing it. At Dundee, the Tay estuary is two miles wide, and the construction linking the railway with Wormit on the opposite bank was regarded by many as a doubtful undertaking. But it was widely admired on its completion. William McGonagall hailed it with his usual ineptitude:

Beautiful Railway Bridge of the Silvery Tay
And prosperity to Messrs. Bouche and Grothe
The famous engineers of the present day who have
        succeeded
in erecting the railway.

There were many who did not share McGonagall's enthusiasm for the beautiful bridge over the river Tay. They were concerned about the effects of strong winds on the high girders in the centre section. On 28 December 1879, their fears proved justified. At 7.20pm that Sunday, when the 5.20 train from Burntisland was making its way across the bridge to Dundee, the storm which had started the previous day reached its peak and swept away the high girders in the centre section together with a thousand feet of the railway line. The storm was 'howling like a banshee' and neither the driver nor the signalman noticed that they were heading for an empty space. Within minutes the entire train plunged into the waters below. Not one of the seventy passengers survived.

When a new bridge was built, McGonagall wrote hopefully:

Beautiful new railway bridge over the silvery Tay
With thy beautiful side screens along your railway
Which will be a great protection on a windy day
So the railway carriages won't blow away...

This second bridge was far more substantial, and is still doing an efficient job today.

It is at Dundee that the river Tay finally reaches the end of its 120-mile journey to the sea. It seems a long way from its source on the slopes of Ben Lui in the heart of Perthshire, a long way from Kenmore and the Birks of Aberfeldy. Beyond the estuary the ocean awaits and Scotland's longest river finally finds its freedom.

THE SOFT LOWLAND TONGUE
OF THE BORDERS

O blythe is the lilt o' his ain mither tongue
To the exile that's lang been roamin'…

If you stand at Carter Bar, the gateway to Scotland, you have magnificent views of the Borders, an area of Scotland known variously for raiders, rugby, wool and Sir Walter Scott — depending on your tastes. But the first time *I* visited the Borders all I wanted to do was enjoy the countryside.

It is indeed a peaceful part of the world, despite the fact that the Borders have a somewhat bloodcurdling history.

You sense some of the turmoil of the past if you attend a game of rugby there. I had watched rugby before I ever visited the area, but it was not until I sat in the stand the day after a concert that I felt such an impassioned atmosphere all around me. The spectators beside me kept rising to their feet either in fury or delight, but I could not see why they were getting so excited. It was only a game, after all.

Naturally such ignorance of the emotions aroused by rugby could not pass unremarked, and my hosts on that occasion took great pains to explain the finer points of the game to me.

The more I travelled round the Borders, the more I began to realize that in towns like Hawick, Galashiels, Melrose and Jedburgh, rugby is not so much a game as a religion. I used to sit at parties surrounded by people who delighted in discussing the latest Samson of the scrum or the rival brave of the back row.

At any rate, I soon became aware that to survive socially in the Borders you have to acquire some knowledge of the game. So I watched, and I listened, and something funny began happening to me on the way to the games. I began to get excited about them.

In fact I got so excited now that my husband says it is more fun watching me than the players, and he is amazed at my fury when the referee gives a decision against my team. Not that I claim to be an expert, but at least I know enough to enjoy every minute of the game.

The rivalry in Borders rugby is so intense that there has to be some deep-seated explanation for it. Perhaps it is that, no longer having English raiders to absorb their aggression, the Borderers have to be content with a good scrap amongst themselves.

But where do the Borders begin and end? To me, Galloway and Dumfries are on the south-west border of Scotland, and the Borders are on the south-east with the river Tweed and its tributaries at the core of an area circled by the Tweedsmuir, Cheviot, Moorfoot and Lammermoor hills.

The exact position of the boundaries may be a subject of debate to this day, but in olden times they were fought over bitterly. Indeed, the whole area was nothing more than a series of competing communities each giving allegiance to their own clan: Kers, Homes, Scotts, Douglases, Elliots, Armstrongs and many others. They had to fight their own battles against the English raiding parties, and when they were not fighting the English they were fighting each other.

Our Border ancestors had to abandon arable farming because their crops were constantly being destroyed by rival clans or the English. Cattle became the local currency, since they could be moved to the safety of deep hollows in the hills — beef tubs — till the raiders had gone. One of the biggest of these is the Devil's Beef Tub just off the Moffat-to-Peebles road.

This is where the Annandale family of Johnstone hid their cattle. There is a story that a fugitive dived into it one misty night to escape his pursuers. He must have been a very brave man: one look over the edge at the sheer drop into the 'tub' was quite enough for me.

Naturally with all this raiding, thieving and murdering going on, both sides had to have lookout posts, so they built 'Peel towers'. These have become as much a feature of the Borders as tweed and rugby.

Jedburgh House, once the home of Mary Queen of Scots, now a fine museum.

'Wasn't there any law and order to protect people?' I once asked a farmer who took me to see the Peel tower on his land.

'Och, well ...' (He scratched his head in some confusion.) 'They had Wardens of the Marches, but they weren't always protective since they sometimes led forays themselves. There were some unwritten laws, mind. For example, if your cattle were stolen, you had the right to go chasing after them for twenty-four hours after the trail was hot. A piece of burning peat at the tip of your lance showed everyone what you were about.'

'And after twenty-four hours?'

'Aye, well... it was every man for himself!' The farmer grinned at the very thought of it. 'Woe betide a Ker if he killed a Home or vice versa. You'd have the whole pack after you then. Mind, they were men of honour in many ways,' he said sagely, 'and they were fiercely loyal to all their clan. A man's word was his bond and there was no hypocrisy — just good dirty fighting.

'The strongest clans ran protection rackets and blackmailed farmers into paying premiums. As

Above Sheepshearing on the Borders. *Right* At the Braw Lads' Gathering, Galashiels, a week-long festival of ceremony and revelry.

long as they kept handing out the money their houses and cattle were safe. They were all at it: the Scotts, the Homes, Elliots, Armstrongs...'

'And the Andersons?' I ventured.

'No Andersons.'

I suppose that is something to be thankful about.

One television series I enjoyed very much was *The Borderers,* and as a child I loved to listen to the ballads about the Border reivers. Some of them are quite romantic. My favourite is 'Muckle-mou'ed Meg' ('big-mouthed Margaret').

Poor Meg. She was a nice girl but she was not exactly in the running for Miss World — or Miss Anything. She was plain and had a large mouth and her father despaired of anyone ever marrying her. Meg had given up hope too until handsome Wat of Harden, one of the Border reivers, passed by on a thieving foray and was captured by Meg's father, Murray of Elibank. Wat was given his choice: hang, or marry muckle-mou'ed Meg. Young Wat took one look at Meg and was

ungallant enough to say he would rather hang. Luckily he changed his mind at the last moment and married her. He kept his word on that like a good Borderer.

The sequel to the story should be that they lived unhappily ever after, but, as it turned out, it was quite the reverse. Meg proved such a gentle, loving wife that handsome Wat saw her inner beauty and fell in love with her.

Incidentally, seeing inner beauty is not easy, as I know to my cost, for I have often been a judge at beauty contests. I hate to see the disappointed looks of the girls who lose. Do not be deceived by all these beaming beauties on television — there are often tears behind the smiles of the losers.

Perhaps the most stirring traditional events in the Borders are the Common Ridings and Festivals, and I was delighted when I was asked to sing at a concert and officiate at the Braw Lads Gathering at Galashiels.

The Vale of Yarrow.

I thought I had better spend five minutes reading up about the Common Ridings before I went, but as it turned out, five minutes was slightly wide of the mark. Let me warn you, if you want to be fully informed about the Common Ridings, set aside five days and prepare to drink plenty of black coffee to keep your strength up.

In May at West Linton there is something called the Whipman Play. In June there are Common Ridings at Hawick and Selkirk. Then there is the Beltane Festival at Peebles. In July there is the Duns 'Reivers Week'. Jethart have their Callants Week, Kelso have a Civic Week, Lauder have a Common Riding and the season of pageantry ends in August with the Coldstream Civic Week.

These are very far from being glorified funfairs. In every case the elaborate pageantry is directly linked to the area's past and the ancient pagan festivals, and events are staged with painstaking care.

There is certainly something pagan about the ceremony of 'Cleikin' the Deil' (catching the Devil) at Innerleithen, in which the devil is caught with a bishop's crook. Before the various roles are cast, there is a tremendous rivalry among the locals. And it goes without saying that more people want to be the devil than the bishop.

Innerleithen itself is one of those delightful Border towns well known for its woollen industry. It is in a lovely setting, where the Leithen Water meets the River Tweed.

Peebles, also famed for its knitwear and tweed, is another town where the river teems

its festival. On Beltane Day the Cornet, the principal figure in the pageant, and his Lass, ride round the town and one of the local school-children is crowned Beltane Queen.

The festivities begin with a church service, then the ceremony of Riding the Marches (the boundaries) takes place. The revellers ride out to Neidpath on the Tweed, where the Warden of the Castle (Neidpath Castle) welcomes them and speeds them on their way back to town.

Another peaceful spot with a stirring festival is Selkirk, a tweed-making town on the edge of the Ettrick Forest which overlooks Ettrick Water. Selkirk was once famed for its souters (shoemakers). At the Common Riding in June only a true 'souter' (someone born in the town) can be the Standard-bearer, because it was a souter who carried back the banner from the battle of Flodden when the English defeated the Scots.

The highpoint of the Festival Week is the casting of the colours, when the Standard-bearer waves the burgh flag round his head before gently lowering it to commemorate that day in 1513 when the 'flowers of the forest' — a whole generation of Borderers — died in battle. It is said that the original souter who brought the news was too distressed to speak and that is why he lowered the flag — to let the people know the tragic news.

Dool and wae for the order sent our lads to the
            border.
The English for once by guile won the day
The flowers of the forest that fought aye the
            foremost
The prime o' our land now lie cauld in the clay.

We'll hear nae mair liltin' at the ewe milkin'
Women and bairns are dowie and wae
Sighin' and moanin' on ilka green loamin'
The flowers of the forest are a' wede away.

The solemnity of the moment when the flag is lowered is preceded by horse-racing, feasting and games of all kinds. As for any animosity towards the English, who were responsible for killing off the flowers of the forest, that is forgotten, and lots of English people come north especially to see the Selkirk ceremony.

Hawick's festival is more light-hearted because there the people are commemorating a victory, not a defeat. After Flodden, the downcast spirits

with salmon and anglers come from far and near to enjoy some of the best fishing in Scotland.

Like Innerleithen's, Peebles' festival week, the Beltane Fair, has pagan origins. Beltane means Baal-fire, Baal being an ancient fertility god. Beltane originally celebrated the coming of the summer on May Day, when witches and warlocks performed strange rites:

At Beltane when ilk bodie bownis
At Peblis to the play
To hear the singin' and the soundis
The solace suth to say.
By firth and forest furth they found
They graythit them full gay…

Scholars say that the verses were written by Scotland's poet king, James V. They describe how everyone dresses up to come to Peebles for of the inhabitants were raised when a group of callants (youths) defeated an English raiding party and triumphantly bore back the captured pennant to their town centre. The dramatic climax of the Hawick Common Riding is 'The Chase', when the Cornet and his followers race their horses along the route taken by the original callants. The chase is so fast and furious it is quite frightening.

I was thankful that I had been invited only to sing at the Braw Lads pageant at Galashiels. I can tell you I would not have lasted long on one of those mad horse rides.

The Braw Lads Gathering lasts a week, since the good folk of the Borders are sound believers in the adage that if you are going to have a festival you might as well make it long enough to be memorable. It begins on a Sunday when there is the kirking (churching) of the Braw Lad and Lass. And they are braw. The Lad wears black and white breeches, blue bonnet and a sash, the Lass a white coat and breeches. As well as the Braw Lad and Lass there are other principals: the Bearer of the Sod, the Bearer of the Stone, the Bearer of the Red Roses and the Bearer of the White Roses. When I say all six are appointed by the Executive Council, you will realize that this ceremony is not to be taken lightly.

Once everyone knows who is doing what, the fun begins. On Monday they all ride out to Lindean Kirk where the Braw Lad places a wreath on the Preacher's Cross. The wreath is hardly laid before rowdy horse-races are staged at Nether Barns. The following evening there is a solemn ride out to Torwoodlea to cut a sod and take a stone from the lands of Ettrick Forest.

Somewhere in the middle of all this I seem to remember a Fancy Dress parade, a civic reception for overseas guests (there appear to be thousands of them) and, on Friday, the Investiture of the Braw Lad and Lass.

Saturday is the grand climax. That is the day when the Braw Lad receives the Burgh Flag and rides out with his supporters to the Englishman's Syke, which is where a band of English soldiers were killed by some braw lads of Galashiels while sitting down to eat some wild plums. The braw lads made a good job of the killing, it seems, because the stream is said to have run with blood for three days. (I warned you that the Borders have had a bloodcurdling past.)

In remembrance of their bravery on that day, the Braw Lass decorates the Braw Lad with a sprig of leaves from the nearby plum trees, her attendants decorate their partners, and the drama is played out against a background of music. Then the whole party sets off to cross the river Tweed and visit Abbotsford, the home of Sir Walter Scott, where they are presented with roses and given a welcoming stirrup cup. Then they return across the Tweed again and ride to the Mercat Cross, where the red and white roses are laid beside the thistle on the cross to commemorate the marriage of Margaret Tudor to James IV.

This marriage was very important for Scotland because it led eventually to the Union of the Crowns. The ride out concludes with an act of homage at the War Memorial, where the flag is dipped in memory of the men of Galashiels who gave their lives in two world wars. The ceremony is simple but impressive and ends when the clock strikes twelve and the Braw Lad returns the flag to the President.

My part in the day's activities was to sing, and I joined in the local hymn of praise to the youth of the district:

Braw Braw Lads on Yarrow Braes
Ye wander through the blooming heather,
But Yarrow Braes nor Ettrick shaws
Can match the lads o' Gala Water.
Braw Braw lads.

Every Border town has its own festival song praising the beauty of its area: Bonnie Lauderdale, Bonnie Langholm, Bonnie Kelso. In Peebles they urge you to 'Come over the hills to Peebles', in Melrose they all sing 'Here's to Melrose' and Hawick sings of 'Teribus the Border Queen'.

I have been to all the Border towns and I am not going to put my head on the chopping block by saying which I prefer, but I can tell you that I was first attracted to them for all the wrong reasons.

The minute a radio or television producer told his cast that we were going on location to the Borders, the girls' eyes would light up. To us a visit to the Borders meant a chance to visit some of the knitwear factories. In the history of Selkirkshire, there is a song of Galashiels which tells all about it:

Abbotsford, Sir Walter Scott's home, which he developed from a run-down farmhouse.

Sing my bonny, harmless sheep
That feed upon the mountains steep,
Bleating sweetly as ye go
Through the winter's frost and snow.

Hart and hind and fallow deer
Not by half as useful are.
Frae king to him that hauds the plough
All are obliged to Tarry Woo'.

Tarry Woo' is ill to spin,
Card it weel ere ye begin,
When tis carded, rowed and spun,
Then the work is halfing done.

But when woven drest and clean
It may be cleading for a queen.

A rough translation would be: you get wool from sheep, you get tweed from wool and then you will be dressed like a queen.

Only after the wool from the sheep has been carded, rolled and spun is it taken to the tweed mills, where it is wound on to pirns for weaving on the rollers. It is a very complicated process, and colour charts showing the number of threads to be used have to be meticulously followed. The end result is beautiful knitwear and tweeds.

Hawick and Galashiels are the two main tweed-mill towns and there is as much rivalry regarding the quality of the tweeds and woollens they produce as there is in their local festivals.

After we had browsed through the mills and begun exploring the countryside, we found there was one thing which unites all Borderers: a love of horses.

Like rugby, horse-riding has its origins in the past, when land-owners had to ride out regularly to check their boundaries and protect their property from invaders. Today the Riding of the Marches preserves this continuity and ensures that there are more horses in this part of Scotland than anywhere else. The youngsters who want to take part in the cavalcades and rides out realize that they will not be eligible for them unless they can ride really well, so every ambitious young Borderer agitates to have riding lessons and, if possible, to own a horse as well.

Certainly it is a stirring sight at the Galashiels Braw Lads festival to see the Ceremonial Ride across the River Tweed to Abbotsford, home of

the most famous Borderer of all, and it seems fitting that it is a direct descendant of Scott who gives the Braw Lad and his Lass the wine and roses of welcome.

I knew all about Sir Walter Scott, of course. In my childhood we had had a full set of Scott's Waverley novels in our bookcase at home which were often taken out and read. Most schools in Scotland had at least one of Scott's novels amongst their list of 'books to be read at home' and we had to study his narrative poems 'The Lay of the Last Minstrel', 'The Lady of the Lake' and 'Marmion' for our examinations. This was no hardship. The verse galloped like the Border horses.

Dying wool at Hawick, one of the many Border towns where the woollen industry predominates.

Day set on Norham's castled steep,
And Tweed's fair river, broad and deep,
    And Cheviot's mountains lone:
The battled towers, the donjon keep,
The looped grates, where captives weep,
The flanking walls that round it sweep,
    In yellow lustre shone.

Of the novels, *The Bride of Lammermuir* perhaps means most to me, since Donizetti's opera *Lucia di Lammermoor* is based on it. Hearing Joan Sutherland sing the title role at Covent Garden was a thrilling experience for me. The role of Lucia, in the *bel canto* style which Joan Sutherland revived so brilliantly, is one of the most technically demanding in the repertoire.

The characters in the story are colourful and romantic — rather like Sir Walter Scott himself, aptly named the 'Wizard of the North'. Small wonder that I grew up in awe of this legendary figure. He not only had a successful career as a Sheriff, a poet, and a novelist, he also set out to achieve a 'mission impossible' which really caught my imagination. He saw a small, neglected farm known as Cartleyhole and, just as Wat of Harden saw the hidden beauty of his bride 'Muckle-mou'ed Meg', so Scott saw the possibilities of the farm. He dreamed of making it into one of the most beautiful houses in Scotland.

Anyone who has ever visited Abbotsford must be staggered by Scott's achievements. Every penny he earned was sunk into Abbotsford. The more successful he became, the more grandiose became his plans for his dream home.

Now, what was once a broken-down cottage is a magnificent turretted mansion with stately rooms, splendid fireplaces, panelled halls, a library and a study. In some of the rooms Scott's personal possessions lie just as he left them and you have the uncanny feeling that the great man could walk in the door any moment.

The irony of Scott's story is that his dream home could be described as the indirect cause of his death. When he was fifty-five a publishing venture in which he had invested failed, and he was left owing creditors a vast sum of money. Yet rather than sell his beloved Abbotsford, Scott decided to pay his debts through his writing. For six years he wrote practically night and day, and succeeded in paying off £80,000 — no mean sum today, but a fortune in the early nineteenth century. At the cost of his health, he managed to preserve the dream mansion, his 'Delilah'.

I suppose the practical side of my Scottish heritage makes me feel it was folly to be so obsessed with a house, but any such feeling is soon dispelled when you visit the place. If his ghost paces the panelled halls, he must be happy to hear the visitors' exclamations of delight.

From Abbotsford's grandeur to the pageantry of the Border festivals, there is a great deal for visitors to enjoy in the Border region, but the impression that remains with me most strongly is of a strong and heart-warming community spirit, so much in contrast to the area's turbulent past, that makes this part of Scotland unique.

Wha but loes the bonnie hills
Wha but loes the shinin' rills
Aye for thee my bosom fills
Bonnie Gallowa'.

It might well be claimed that ex-world champion racing driver Jackie Stewart has been the best publicist for Scotland since the invention of tartan and Scotch whisky. I would be inclined to go along with that. Whenever he was competing in a Grand Prix I watched him on television, holding my breath as he negotiated the hairpin bends and feeling incredibly proud when the announcer declared that Scotland's Jackie Stewart was the winner.

Watching all those Grand Prix events must have had their effect, because I admit there is a bit of Jackie Stewart in my make-up — which might come as a surprise to those who see me in a more demure light. The facts are that whenever I sing at engagements in England or Wales, I rarely stay overnight; even if the concert does not finish till after eleven, there is nothing I like better than to get behind the wheel of my car and go zooming up the motorway back home to Scotland.

On the journey north, reaching the border is one of the highlights of the journey. Some foolhardy folk say the Borders stretch from the east coast to the west, but there is a fairly strict distinction between 'the Borders' in the south-east (which include such towns as Gala, Hawick and Jedburgh) and the south-west, comprising Galloway and Dumfries, where the chief towns are Stranraer, Kirkcudbright and, of course, the county town Dumfries.

Strangely enough, the best-known spot on that borderland between Scotland and England is not a big town, but a little village called Gretna Green. Its fame rests on the fact that because an old Scots law allowed couples to marry at the age of sixteen without their parents' consent, and Gretna Green was the first village over the Scottish border, there was until quite recently a steady stream of young runaway lovers arriving in the village to get married — in vehicles that ranged from sleek limousines to battered old heaps.

Gretna became a mecca for runaway couples not just because the age qualification for marriage was higher in other countries but because in Scotland you did not have to be married by a minister of the church or at a registry office until 1940. All you had to do was to declare in front of two witnesses that you wanted to be married and a 'priest' (no religious connection — just the name for the local man performing the ceremony) would marry you. Over the anvil in the blacksmith's shop was the most popular place for the ceremony, although anywhere would do as long as someone was there to officiate.

Time was of the essence at those Gretna nuptials, since the runaway lovers were often pursued by angry parents hoping to stop the wedding before it had a chance to take place; either the man or the woman would have to have lived in Scotland for three weeks before they could be legally married there.

There are many stories of colourful chases through the village streets, tearful daughters being pulled into cars by angry fathers, and lovers hiding in the nearby woods hoping to make a dash to the blacksmith's shop before their pursuers spotted them. Many such incidents have made newspaper headlines over the years, especially if either of the lovers concerned were rich and famous — as indeed they often were.

Nowadays the laws have changed. Today, you have to be married in a church or registry office, but you do not have to stay in Gretna to establish residence. All you have to do is write for a Marriage Notice, fill it in and send it in to the Register at Gretna. The Notice is displayed on a public board for fourteen days and after that you can get married, even if you arrive the night before the wedding.

Despite the changes in the law, however, the legend lingers on and couples are still coming from faraway places to plight their troth. Such is Gretna's fame that it attracts over a quarter of a million visitors every year.

Outside Annie Laurie's house near Moniaive in the Cairn Valley, Dumfriesshire.

Gretna is no longer the first village you reach when you cross the border because the A74 by-passes it, yet I always think of those runaway romances when I pass through the area.

The newspapers used to print articles about the romantic places in Dumfries and Galloway which newlyweds might wish to visit on their honeymoons. From reading those, I came to know the region's history, together with many of its myths and legends.

Thinking about them helps to pass the time on a long car-journey home from the south. A few hundred yards away from the farm buildings of old Gretna stands the Clochmaben Stone, supposed to have been the site of a secret meeting-place in ancient times.

About fifteen miles away, at the southern end of Castle Loch, stands Lochmaben Castle, which managed to withstand several sieges in the fifteenth and sixteenth centuries and was once visited by Mary Queen of Scots. Is now a ruin, but

The blacksmith's shop at Gretna Green - scene of many a furtive wedding and a popular tourist attraction.

it is fun to weave fantasies about what life was like in those days.

For Gretna couples, however, I think the most enchanting place to visit must be Eskdalemuir, where they were still holding 'handfasting fairs' in the eighteenth century. After holding hands at a public ceremony at one of these fairs, a couple could embark on a trial marriage for a year. If the trial was not successful, they came back to the fair the following year and admitted their failure. I think it was an appalling idea: private post mortems for marital breakdowns are bad enough, public ones an embarrassment.

Not so far from Eskdalemuir lived a woman who was so devoted to her husband that she refused to be parted from his heart when he died. This was Devorgilla, one of the best-known names in Galloway's history. She was the wife of John Balliol (after whom Balliol College, Oxford is named). When he died, Devorgilla had his heart embalmed and kept it by her side in a silver casket for twenty-one years. On her death, the people of Galloway were so touched by her fidelity that they buried her with her husband in front of the abbey altar and placed the silver casket containing his heart beside her. The place became known as Dolce Cor − sweet heart − and so Sweetheart Abbey got its name. The ruined abbey is an enchanting place to visit.

If you go west from Gretna you come to Dumfries, where Robert the Bruce began his fight for Scottish independence by stabbing the Red Comyn (the English administrator) on the altar steps of Greyfriars church. The minute he committed the crime, he was tortured with doubts. He voiced these doubts to his companion, who replied firmly that he had better 'mak siccar', and promptly stabbed the Red Comyn several times more to make sure he was well and truly dead (a gruesome tale, but it was stirring stuff to read in our history books at school).

Bonnie Prince Charlie was another famous figure who left his mark on Dumfries. In fact you could say he left the citizens a clean pair of heels − because he stole a thousand pairs of shoes for the sore feet of his army, not to mention taking £2,000 and, as a hostage, their Provost.

The grave of the poet who wrote some of the world's most beautiful love songs can also be found at Dumfries: Robert Burns came to live here in 1791, and is buried at St Michael's Church.

Burns had come from his native Ayrshire to Ellisland, near Dumfries, to farm, but the farm was exhausted; despite his progressive methods he failed and was obliged to take a job with the Customs and Excise office. As an exciseman, he would have spent much of his time watching out for the smugglers on the Solway coast and ensuring that duty was paid on excisable liquor. Being an exciseman was not the road to instant popularity, as Burns knew. Typically, he drew on his experience in a lively ballad, 'The Deil's awa wi' the Exciseman'.

Sweetheart Abbey, Kirkcudbright.

We'll mak our maut and we'll brew our drink,
We'll laugh, sing and rejoice, man,
And mony braw thanks to the meikle black deil
That danced awa wi' the Exciseman.

The Mid-Steeple, where Burns' body lay in state before his funeral, is now part of the High Street of Dumfries.

Although it was the Gretna romances which first stimulated my interest in the south-west of Scotland, and it was Burns who furthered it by his exploits in Dumfries, I really came to know the area at first hand through my singing, as I had many invitations to sing at concerts, make radio programmes and do location work for television series.

When filming, we had to start early and work through the day without a break if the weather was good. Frequently, this being Scotland, it was not — and that meant the filming had to stop.

I was never too downhearted when the heavens opened because I was then free to explore the surrounding countryside - and I began to appreciate that Galloway and Dumfries have some of the wildest and least spoiled scenery in Scotland, both inland and along the coast.

Castle Douglas has long been a favourite film location because of its picturesque hills, tree-lined loch and the beautiful gardens of the castle itself. I remember one occasion there when the director decided that I should sing some songs on horseback.

Perhaps his imagination had been fired by the story of Mary Queen of Scots. She reached Galloway by riding sixty miles: quite an endurance test. In Galloway, she had to abandon her horse and take to the hills on foot, wearing a wig over her shaved head as a disguise. She spent her last night in Scotland at Dundrennan Abbey in the Solway Firth. The next morning as she stepped into the boat which she hoped would take her to the safe protection of her cousin Queen Elizabeth, the Archbishop of St Andrews had a premonition that all would not turn out well. He begged Mary to stay in Scotland but she refused, and sailed away to imprisonment and eventual execution in England.

Whether my director was under the impression that my equestrian prowess equalled that of Mary Queen of Scots, I do not know. But it did

The Burns memorial at Dumfries, where Burns lived for the last five years of his life.

not, and that horse somehow knew it. He used every trick in the book to make me feel uncomfortable but he kept the best for last. The camera did not start rolling until my costume, hair and make-up were immaculate and I was poised perfectly on the horse's back. As I reached the climax of my song, I was just congratulating myself on mastering the beast when he suddenly jerked his head forward and sent me sliding down his neck. As far as I know, that episode ended upon the cutting-room floor — a classic 'out-take' if ever there was one.

It was when we were filming in Castle Douglas that I had the chance to renew my acquaintance with Kirkcudbright, a sailing and fishing centre on the Dee estuary. The name Kirkcudbright means 'church of Cuthbert'. The body of this revered saint rested here briefly before being carried on to Durham by the monks of Lindisfarne.

Kirkcudbright is also known as the burial-place of the celebrated gypsy king of Scotland, Billy Marshall. This man fathered four children after the age of 100, fought in battles when he was 102 and lived to the age of 120. No wonder the people of Kirkcudbright look at his grave with awe.

The main streets of the town are a delight. Wandering through them I saw painters, potters and weavers at work in the little eighteenth-century byways. One of my favourite artists, A.E. Hornel, lived in Kirkcudbright in Broughton House, which he later bequeathed to the town. Now a museum, many of his books and paintings can be seen there. My favourite Hornel painting is *Blue Flax*. It shows three little girls in a meadow brimming over with deep-blue flowers. I find the softness of colour and the delicacy in the portrayal of the children's faces very appealing.

Sometimes radio or television work has taken me further to the west of Galloway. Once, during a break in filming, I was standing, hands in pockets, on a hillside when an old shepherd came up and started chatting. He was an interesting old chap and told me that the Romans had once camped on this spot, as had the Picts. The Vikings had beached on the distant shore and so, too, had the Irish monks who wanted to convert the heathen to Christianity.

Before he went away, he advised me not to miss seeing Glen Trool, and this proved good advice indeed. Glen Trool is spectacular: acre upon acre of rolling mountains, glittering lochs, and forests so thick and impenetrable that they reminded me of something out of Grimm's fairy tales. Glen Trool is in the Galloway Forest Park and the wild life is as varied as the scenery. West of Glen Trool is Stranraer, which stands at the head of Loch Ryan. Stranraer has been called the gateway to Scotland from Ireland. When I was with the Kirkintilloch Junior Choir, we were invited to sing in Ireland, and it was at Stranraer that we boarded the ferry for the trip to Larne.

That stretch of water is one of the roughest around Britain, and our crossing was fairly typical. However, although some of the choir looked rather green when they stepped off at Larne, I was unaffected by the experience. I love the sea and the minute the ferry had left Stranraer I had gone up on deck and sung to myself to keep my mind off sea-sickness.

It was the same on the way back, and by the time we returned to Stranraer I felt exhilarated. I have happy memories of those trips to Ireland and was very shocked when that stormy crossing eventually proved too much for the ferry, the *Princess Victoria*. She sank during a great storm in January 1953 in which many lives were lost.

Recently I visited another part of Dumfriesshire: Maxwelton House, near Moniaive, where Annie Laurie was born in 1682. 'Annie Laurie' is one of Scotland's best-known songs:

Maxwelton braes are bonnie
Where early fa's the dew,
And t'was there that Annie Laurie
Gave me her promise true,
Which ne'er forgot will be,
And for bonnie Annie Laurie
I lay me doon and dee.

Annie Laurie's real name was Anna Laurie (only in the song is she called Annie). Anna fell in love with William Douglas of Fingland. It was an unfortunate choice since William was a Jacobite and Anna's father was a Royalist, which made them deadly enemies.

Despite this, the sweethearts contrived to meet secretly on the banks and braes of Maxwelton, and there they exchanged vows of everlasting love. Sadly, the family persisted in refusing to give their approval to the match; then came rumours of a Stuart uprising and William Douglas was forced to flee. The lovers never met again

Overleaf Clatteringshaw's Loch, formed as a result of a dam being built over the river Dee.

and though they each married someone else, the song tells the story of Anna and William's love.

It was Anna's lover William Douglas who wrote the original words, but they were adapted later on by Lady John Scott who decided to change William's stumbling tribute to his sweetheart and make the poem more pleasing. She set her version to a melody she had composed earlier.

I do not sing 'Annie Laurie' because it is a man's song, the story of a man's love for his sweetheart, though I love the music.

The part of Dumfriesshire where Annie 'gave… her promise true' is a region of green valleys, rolling farmlands and sleepy little villages. Moniaive is in the Cairn Valley, where the Cairn Water is formed by the meeting of three sparkling streams: Craigdarroch, Dalwhat and Castlefairn. A few miles away is Annie Laurie's home, Maxwelton House, which on certain days is open to the public. The house no longer belongs to the Laurie family and was in desperate need of restoration when it was bought by the late Hugh Stenhouse in 1968. He made the restoration of the private chapel his first priority, guided perhaps by the Latin quotation (from Psalm 127) above a doorway in the east wing which reads, in translation: 'Except the Lord build the house, they labour in vain that build it.'

A stern warning indeed, and Hugh Stenhouse and his wife paid heed to it. They repaired the altar furnishings, put new carpets on the floor and fresh covers on the hassocks and cushions.

Then they turned their attention to the mansion itself: a formidable task! Sixty-five men worked there for three years, excavating and repairing. They found a beautiful stone chimney-piece at the south end of the dining room, uncovered doorways in the west wing and discovered a vaulted room with three small windows which no one knew existed. Originally this room had been a kitchen and today the old fireplace is in use once more.

When the plaster was stripped from the chimney breasts in the dining room, the arms of Sir Robert Laurie and Jean Riddell, Annie Laurie's parents, were revealed. In another part of the house, a secret room was discovered concealed in the huge chimney breast which rises from the dining room below.

Once the old structures were revealed and repaired, the Stenhouses set about finding carpets, furniture and wall hangings which would enhance the beauty of the house. In the dining room, there is a table of Spanish chestnut and a carpet of Portuguese needlework that they commissioned for the room. In the drawing room the parquet floor was made from the wood of a yew tree which was growing too close to the house.

The same wood was used in the room which has become known as Annie Laurie's boudoir. Her portrait, painted by Alexander Mossman, is just outside the door and inside this charming little room, which has a pleasantly intimate atmosphere, are small needlework tables and a miniature marquetry chest of drawers.

Now, when I listen to the song, I can visualize Annie Laurie sitting in that boudoir or walking on Maxwelton Braes – every bit as 'bonnie' as the song had led me to imagine.

One of my happiest memories of the day I went to see Annie Laurie's home is the time I spent with some sheep-shearers on my way home. They were working away with such obvious pleasure that I had to stop to chat to them.

The sheep-shearers seemed surprised when I admired their skill and asked if I would like to lend a hand, and when they stopped for a tea-break it was taken for granted that I would share in it.

The farmer's wife came bustling down the field carrying a huge tray laden with plates of home-made scones and cakes – rich country fare. She gave me a friendly smile and when one of the men told her who I was, she said, 'The one we see on television?'

'The same,' I replied.

'Och, goodness!' she exclaimed, looking at the mugs on the tray, 'I'll away and get the best china.'

And before I could stop her, she was hurrying up the field back to the house. The men laughed, the sun shone and I felt totally relaxed and content. Bonnie Galloway and Dumfriesshire have much to offer those in search of scenery and history, but it is, after all, the people that count. As I sat there with the sheep-shearers, I was touched by the easy friendship and hospitality I had found – qualities which have endeared Scotland to countless numbers of people every bit as much as her songs.

In the so-called 'boudoir' of Annie Laurie's house at Moniaive.

MY AIN FOLK

Far frae my hame I wander;
But still my thoughts return
To my ain folk ower yonder,
In the sheiling by the burn.

Whenever I hear that Queen Elizabeth the Queen Mother is holidaying at her summer retreat, the Castle of Mey in Caithness, I am vividly reminded of my childhood, for it was to northern Scotland that I used to go with my family each summer to stay with relatives – with 'my ain folk'.

My parents, my two brothers, my sister and I spent our holidays with my Uncle Tom in Brora, Sutherland, and from there we explored Caithness to the north and Easter Ross to the south. The whole of the northern Highlands became our playground. Caithness and Sutherland are often called the 'big country' because they encompass 2,400 square miles of rivers, lochs and mountains bounded by a rugged coastline. Along this coast, small fishing villages hug the headlands and sea birds plummet from high cliffs such as the ones at Dunnet Head. Inland lie heathered moors, strange rock formations and high mountains which are the haunt of the golden eagle.

To the south of Brora the old county of Ross stretches across the Highlands from coast to coast. The climate is mild, thanks to the Gulf Stream, and the scenery ranges from beautiful inland lochs to castles which stand beside humble crofts. The joy of Ross is its contrast: modesty and magnificence go hand in hand.

In our family the summer holiday excitement began at Easter. Soon after, we began counting the days till *the* day arrived. For weeks we would debate which clothes to take, and what we would do when we arrived there. Not surprisingly we rarely slept the night before we left. I used to lie in bed willing away the hours until morning.

Today, delays at airports and railway stations are a cause of frustration for everyone. But then, for us, the journey was half the fun – and it was quite a journey. We left Kirkintilloch in the early morning to travel to Glasgow's Buchanan Street Station where the north-bound train awaited us.

Since the railway carriage was to be 'home' for many hours, we devised various ploys for discouraging strangers from joining us. The first small battle was to get a carriage to ourselves, then came the competition for the window seats. When I see children today setting off on long journeys armed with toys, books, puzzles and sweets, I cannot help smiling. My mother would have none of that. She took the view that we were lucky to be there and we ought to sit back and enjoy what the journey itself had to offer. I am very grateful to her now because it made us appreciate that incredibly beauiful scenery.

One of the first high points of the journey was Stirling, the gateway to the Highlands. If it was going to be a good day, Stirling was often shrouded in heat haze, which added to the enchantment of the shadowy buildings surrounded by the Links of Forth. Yet it was not so much the town that fascinated us as the castle. From the train, we would gaze up at the 250-foot rock surmounted by Stirling Castle, dominating the landscape for miles around.

Many years later when I visited Stirling Castle, I realized that the view looking down from the battlements is even more impressive than the one looking up from the train. From the battlements' lofty heights there is a panoramic view of the town, the river and the magnificent peaks of the mountains to the north, among them Ben Lomond, Ben Venue, Ben Ledi and Ben More.

Five famous battlefields can be seen from the castle: Stirling Bridge, Bannockburn, Sauchieburn, Falkirk and Sheriffmuir. It was William Wallace who routed the English at the Battle of Stirling Bridge and you can see the towering Wallace Monument on the far side of the Forth. In the distance too you can see the field of Bannockburn where Scotland's most famous warrior, Robert the Bruce, defeated Edward II. It was this battle which established him as King of Scotland.

Duncansby stacks, just off the coast of John o' Groats. The 'last house' can be seen in the distance.

After Stirling the next eagerly awaited station was Perth because it was here that we could stretch our legs and buy mugs of railway tea to accompany our picnic. By that time nothing could have been more welcome.

From Perth the train sped northwards. Dunkeld, Pitlochry, Blair Atholl, Kingussie and Aviemore flashed past. In those days there was no Aviemore complex, no ski lifts, no hotels; and, since we journeyed north in summer, neither was there any snow.

Before too long we reached Inverness, the capital of the Highlands, with its silvery river and backdrop of woods and mountains. Here we changed trains for the last leg of our journey to Brora on the north-east coast.

We followed a circuitous route past the peninsulas formed by the Beauly, Cromarty and Dornoch Firths, and, since our destination lay to the east, we were filled with indignation when the train swung westward to the inland town of Lairg. By the time we arrived there we had been in the train a full six hours and were desperate to reach our journey's end.

Above Remembering many a childhood ramble. *Right* Beyond the bright carpet of heather lie the peaceful waters of Dornoch Firth.

From Lairg to Golspie seemed the longest part of the journey but our spirits rose on catching a glimpse of the statue of the first Duke of Sutherland which stands on the hill outside the town. Then came the spectactular Dunrobin Castle, seat of the Dukes of Sutherland, which resembles a French château and looks like something out of a fairytale.

The next stop was Brora, at last, and when we finally tumbled out of our carriage we had been

travelling for more than eight hours. But our tiredness was forgotten as we raced along the platform to meet Uncle Tom. By the time we had reached his house, unpacked and had a meal, exhaustion had usually caught up with us. That first night was one night in the year when there were no disputes when my mother announced it was bedtime.

The next morning we would wake early and run out into the garden to make sure nothing had changed. We were never disappointed. There was the beautiful sandy bay stretching for miles, and the sea sparkling in the morning light. Along the shore was the golf course and around us were hills and glens waiting to be explored.

Since my uncle's house was outside Brora, we children enjoyed our trips into the village every morning to collect milk, bread and other necessities. Even that was an adventure for us, and we would often linger at the small harbour from which the first settlers left for New Zealand after the Highland Clearances.

After the shopping, the day was ours and we always made full use of it. Sometimes we would bathe in one of the nearby sandy bays, and if we were not swimming, we would go looking for shells or exploring the pools left by the tide.

The boys were always wanting us to hunt for worms for their fishing (the river Brora teems with salmon). The most exciting time to walk along the river bank was at night, when we would sometimes see lights glowing in the dark, betraying the presence of poachers. We would stand and watch, then suddenly rush away in sheer fright in case we were discovered. The poachers were probably very angry because the noise we made would undoubtedly have frightened away any fish around.

Four miles up the river is Loch Brora, dominated by the 700-foot-high Carrol Rock. Right at the head of the loch is a broch built by the Picts, of whom there are several reminders in this area. In Kintradwell, for example, there is a drystane tower which archaeologists say was used for fortification in 200 BC.

Uncle Tom told us a lot about these local sites and also about the nearby coal mine, dating from 1529 and the oldest in Scotland. Sadly the mine is closed now, but more recently Brora's industry has produced another claim to fame: its distillery produces a peat-flavoured whisky called Clyneleish, much sought after by connoisseurs and locals alike.

One of the diversions we most enjoyed as children was to go to Winnie Sutherland's croft. Half of the people in the village were Sutherlands, and Winnie's croft had been handed down through many generations of the same family. No doubt she found running the place very hard work, but we loved feeding the hens and collecting the eggs. Best of all we liked helping with the hay, though I am quite sure we were more of a hindrance than a help.

Another magnet which drew us was Don (Sutherland, of course), the local weaver. His simple workshop had frames for weaving and wheels on which he spun his wool. We thought it magical to see his hands moving so swiftly and surely, for undoubtedly he was an expert at his craft and people came from far and wide to buy his tweeds and tartan rugs. Sometimes the Duke and Duchess of Sutherland would bring visitors to watch him working and to purchase something from him. The news would spread and we would race down and press our noses against the window to see the grand folk who lived in the fairytale castle. The minute they left, we would rush in and ask Don what the Duke and Duchess had said. Like most Highlanders, Don had that easy, nonchalant manner which made him treat everyone alike. He was surprised by our interest in the Duke and Duchess, but for our part we could not understand why he was not more impressed by his grand visitors.

Years later I visited Dunrobin Castle, and like all who see it I was not disappointed. The setting, on a natural terrace by the sea, is superb, and I remember thinking that it looked slightly unreal, almost like a mirage. Yet the castle walls are massive, especially those of the old Keep which stands four storeys high with no permanent stair. According to legend, the severed head of a rebel claimant to the earldom was once displayed at the top.

Inside the castle are large, impressive rooms with fine furniture and tapestries. On the walls of the drawing-room hang two large paintings by Canaletto and a set of eighteenth-century Mortlake tapestries. There are family portraits, Louis XV furniture and a ceiling which bears the Sutherland coat of arms. Trophies, and the regimental colours of the 93rd Sutherland Highlanders, who formed the thin red line at the battle of Balaclava, are displayed in the entrance hall and on the main staircase. Certainly Dunrobin is well worth a visit.

Glass-blowing at the Caithness Glass factory in Wick, an activity that has never failed to fascinate me.

One of our favourite excursions from Brora was south to Dornoch, the old capital of Sutherland. Here there are a thirteenth-century cathedral and an ancient castle which is now an hotel, but the main attractions of Dornoch as a holiday resort are its beautiful golf courses, fine sands and good fishing – both sea and freshwater.

South of Dornoch is Dingwall on the Cromarty Firth. Some people may have heard of Dingwall in connection with air travel, because it was there that the Scots airline Loganair started. On one of our summer holiday trips to Brora, we stayed for a few days in Dingwall. We walked along the banks of the river Conon and sometimes climbed the hills to the south of the town where there is a tower commemorating the birth of a famous soldier, General Sir Hector Macdonald.

Dingwall also recalls for me the stories about the Brahan Seer, perhaps the most famous prophet Scotland has ever produced. The Brahan

Dunrobin Castle, once a thirteenth-century square keep but extensively altered in 1856.

Seer was a man called Kenneth Mackenzie, born on the island of Lewis. He left Lewis to work for his cousin on his farm at Brahan near Dingwall. His cousin's wife disliked him so intensely she decided to murder him by poisoning his lunch. She did not know that on the very day she had picked Kenneth had fallen asleep on a fairy knoll, and when he awoke he found himself clutching a fairy stone which allowed him to see into the future. He knew instantly what his cousin's wife

intended and threw the poisoned food away. This was the beginning of the legend of his second sight, that strange gift which is attributed to so many Highlanders. As children, we were fascinated by this local story.

In later years, we stayed with friends at nearby Strathpeffer. The Brahan Seer had made certain prophecies about Strathpeffer many years before. Speaking of the town's well he said: 'Uninviting and disagreeable as it now is with its thick, crusted surface and unpleasant smell, the day shall come when it shall be under lock and key, and crowds of pleasure-seekers and health-seekers shall be seen thronging its portals in their eagerness to get a draught of its waters.'

No one believed him, but − amazingly − his prophecy came true. Mineral springs were discovered in the district and it became a well-known spa.

The villagers of Strathpeffer are making sure that the Brahan Seer's other prophecy does not come true. He predicted that when the old carved stone standing on the outskirts of the village had fallen three times, the village would vanish under a flood. Not many of the villagers will admit to believing the prophecy, but through the years local people have made sure that the carved stone is so strongly reinforced that it has no chance of falling.

One place we visited as children was Beauly, a name derived from 'beau lieu', French for 'beautiful place'. Beauly deserves such a name, for it has purple hills rising behind it and the gentle waters of the Beauly Firth lapping its feet. The day we visited Beauly there was great excitement because King George VI and Queen Elizabeth were paying a visit to the local shop to purchase their favourite tweeds. Everyone crowded round the entrance, including ourselves. A real live king just a few feet away from us! I was about ten at the time and remember suffering the inevitable childish disappointment that the king was not wearing his crown.

The majority of our day-trips from Brora took us to the north. Lairg, which lay west of Loch Brora, was a good centre for excursions farther afield. From Lairg buses ran to and from Lochinver, Scourie, Kinlochbervie, Durness, Tongue and Bettyhill.

It is on the Lairg-to-Tongue road that one is likely to meet overseas visitors looking for traces

of their ancestors, since it was from the Strath Naver district in particular that many crofters were evicted at the time of the infamous Highland Clearances, when many landlords, having decided that sheep were more profitable than people, compelled their tenants to take ship for distant lands.

Yet though they left their native land, they never forgot it and they have handed down tales about it from generation to generation. Today, the old grudges have long since been forgotten and Americans, Australians and New Zealanders can be seen wandering around the area's ruined crofts imagining what life must have been like for their distant forebears. To me it is very heartening to see how proud these people are of their Scottish ancestry.

From Tongue the road curves round Loch Eriboll, a remote and beautiful spot where grey seals abound. Spectacular caves can be found farther west at Sango Bay where the Caves of Smoo rise to 120 feet high and stretch for 200 yards. A rushing waterfall completes this dramatic picture — one which much impressed Sir Walter Scott when he went there in 1814.

Sango Bay is near Durness, where a service road leads to the lighthouse on Cape Wrath, the extreme north-west point of the Scottish mainland. The area around Durness is one of the few places where you can still hear Gaelic spoken, though it is only a second language.

Of all the places in the north of Scotland surely the most famous in John o' Groats. We used to travel there up the road from Brora, which passed through Helmsdale then up and over the great expanse of the Ord of Caithness. From there it went down to the little village of Berriedale before starting to climb once more and to negotiate the hairpin bends which eventually led to Wick.

Close to Wick, the county town of Caithness, is the famous Caithness glass factory, which was originally started there to help unemployment. Local workers were trained by skilled craftsmen brought in from abroad and eventually the Caithness Glass Company developed a coloured glass cased in clear crystal. The surrounding countryside is said to have inspired the beautiful moss green, twilight blue, peat and heather colours which have given Caithness glass its international reputation. It was so fascinating to watch the men glass-blowing that we had to make quite

The calm waters of Loch Stack, just north of Achfary, with Ben Stack visible in the background.

an effort to tear ourselves away in order to press on to John o' Groats.

Although Dunnet Head is actually the most northerly point, John o' Groats has acquired the reputation of being 'the Land's End of Scotland'. People flock to be photographed outside the white-washed fisherman's cottage which is repu-tedly the last house in Britain. Inevitably, and sadly, the cottage has become a souvenir shop.

Some people are disappointed that there is so little to see at John o' Groats, just an hotel, a scat-tering of houses and flat countryside where cone-shaped haystacks are held down with ropes and stones. But the beauty of John o' Groats lies in its

Wester Ross, near the remote hamlet of Achiltibuie.

sea view. On a sunny day, the sun glints in the green fields and cliffs of the Orkney Islands opposite, the strange, isolated Old Man of Hoy to the left and South Ronaldsay to the right. To the east there are the famous stacks of Duncansby: great sandstone obelisks aggressively thrusting up from the wild waters of the Pentland Firth.

The waves on this northern coast are amazing, and sometimes so wild that stones flung from the sea have broken windows on the Duncansby Head lighthouse, 346 feet above.

Between the Orkney Isles and John o' Groats is the Isle of Stroma, once well known locally for witches who had the evil eye. At one time, if a fisherman met a local witch on his way to his boat, he would turn on his heel and go staight back to his cottage. If she had put the evil eye on him, his boat would capsize and he would drown. A silly superstition? Perhaps, but the local fisherman were not willing to risk it.

Near Stroma is the Swelchie whirlpool. This, too, has a legend attached to it. A monster is supposed to live in the Swelchie, and when he reaches out to clutch at unwary sailors, their only hope of placating him is to throw him their cargo.

On such a wild and seemingly danger-ridden coastline, it seems strange to turn back and look at inland landscapes which are more reminiscent of the flat fields of Holland. Perhaps it is appropriate that the name 'John o' Groats' is reputed to be the anglicized name of a Dutchman who annoyed the local magistrate by charging too much for the ferry fare to Orkney. The magistrate decided to curb the Dutchman's greed by fixing the fee at one groat.

John de Groot had other problems, too — namely eight sons who fought over who should take precedence in his home. The wily Dutchman settled the dispute by building an octagonal house with a door on each of the eight sides and a large octagonal table in the middle. In this way no son could say that he had precedence. It is such an extraordinary story that it could well be true. The building, unfortunately, has disappeared, and in its place stands a modern hotel.

Not far from John o' Groats is Dunnet Head, the *real* northern tip of Scotland, where the cliffs soar like skyscrapers and the sea foams and swirls in a white angry rage. And between these two rival Land's Ends stands the Castle of Mey. This was the seat of the Earl of Caithness until the Queen Mother bought it in 1952. Some people think it strange that she should have chosen such a wild, isolated spot for her holiday home, but they can only be those who have never seen the variety and rugged grandeur of Scotland's northern shorelines — the very coast I came to know and love through our summer holidays in Brora.

AE FOND KISS

Ae fond kiss, and then we sever, —
Ae fareweel, and then — for ever,
Deep in the heart-wrung tears I'll pledge thee!
Warring sighs and groans I'll wage thee!

Spring in Edinburgh, and the trees beside Princes Street rustle in the breeze. Is there a more dramatic promenade anywhere in the world? The lovely street is bordered on one side by beautifully kept gardens rising to rugged crags, on which stands a spectacular castle. Straining upwards towards the castle are the towering eight-storey houses and steeples of the Royal Mile, named in honour of the kings and queens who walked there.

When the sun parts the clouds on a dull day and gleams on the crags and the castle, it seems like a setting for one of Wagner's operas and, as if to emphasize the drama, at one o'clock a gun booms out over the city, giving the citizens a time-check while at the same time perhaps reminding them of Edinburgh's stormy past.

Since Edinburgh is less than an hour's journey from Glasgow, I am a frequent visitor to both the Old Town, stretching from Edinburgh Castle to the Palace of Holyroodhouse and to the 'New Town' which was begun in the eighteenth century when the growth of Edinburgh could no longer be contained within the Flodden Wall, built as a defensive measure after Scotland's defeat at Flodden. The draining of the Nor' Loch (now Princes Street Gardens) began a process which continued until Edinburgh became one of the most beautiful cities in Europe, with the rich and famous moving from the narrow confines of old Edinburgh to the spacious houses of George Street and Queen Street.

I love attending official functions in the eighteenth-century New Town because they are usually held in places such as Bute House, the residence of the Secretary of State, in Charlotte Square. This is one of the lovely squares in Edinburgh in which the gracious Georgian houses bring back the elegance of a bygone age. Sir Compton Mackenzie, one of Scotland's most celebrated writers, used to live in Drummond Place, another lovely square.

One of my favourite streets in Edinburgh, Ann Street, lies outside the New Town across the Water of Leith. Its great attraction is the doll-like scale of the buildings. The painter Henry Raeburn gave the street to his wife as a birthday present. 'Follow that!' you might say.

My earliest memories of summer in Edinburgh are of childhood visits to Edinburgh Zoo, one of the best in Britain, and to the National Museum of Antiquities, where we could see momentoes of celebrated figures from Scottish history.

I remember being taken to the Grassmarket and to Greyfriars Church, where the National Covenant, a solemn undertaking to oppose the evils of the Anglican faith imposed on Scotland by Charles I, was signed in 1638. This is also the location of the Greyfriars Bobby statue. Greyfriars Bobby was the Skye terrier who was so devoted to his master that he stood guard over his grave for fourteen years. The people of Edinburgh fed him during all that time and Baroness Coutts was so impressed by his long vigil that after his death in 1872 she erected a statue to him. I loved the story of Greyfriars Bobby as a child, and still do. I often think of it when I look at my own faithful dog, Jimmy, who follows me wherever I go.

When I first went to Edinburgh to sing, it was with the Kirkintilloch Junior Choir, and our audience consisted of the church dignitaries who had gathered in the Assembly Hall of the Church of Scotland. The Assembly Hall is at the top of the Mound, the street which was constructed from the rubble resulting from the building of the New Town. The Mound now divides Princes Street Gardens into east and west.

Since singing with the choir took up only part of the day, the rest of it was spent sightseeing. Friends and relatives showed me around too, and I remember visits to the old Royal High School (where, at a later date, I was to sing), modelled on the Temple of Theseus in Athens,

Edinburgh's Royal Mile: a typical section showing the old, low-ceilinged buildings.

and to that other Greek-style structure, the unfinished 'Parthenon' on Calton Hill. When I was taken to the 'other' Assembly Rooms in George Street I was suitably impressed to hear that Gladstone, Charles Dickens and William Thackeray had lectured there, and Paderewski had given piano recitals.

Spring and early summer in Edinburgh are delightful, but the city really comes to life in August, when Princes Street is crowded with visitors to the Edinburgh Festival. The eagerness with which international stars accept invitations to appear there is a measure of the Festival's prestige. The events include concerts, operas, ballets, plays and art exhibitions.

And then of course there is 'The Fringe', the unofficial offshoot of the Festival in which informality and experiment are the order of the day. You can spend an hour attending a Fringe concert and be confronted by a juggler, artist or musician performing on the pavement as you leave. Hundreds of artists head for the Festival Fringe each year. They include companies from every part of the world, all hoping for the kind of fame and fortune which came the way of, for example, David Frost or the original *Beyond the Fringe* cast, who were so successful there in the early years of their careers.

Early in my career as a professional singer, I sang for two consecutive years in the *Edinburgh Fancy,* a revue of songs, dancing and poetry. I felt wonderful wearing the lovely period dresses and I still have some photographs to remind me of those happy occasions.

Accommodation is always difficult to find at Festival times, but I was specially fortunate to be staying with Margaret and Jim Hunter. Margaret is a small, dark-haired bundle of energy who is a founder member of the Edinburgh Festival Voluntary Guides Association, a band of unpaid enthusiasts who take visitors on guided tours of the Royal Mile. If visitors offer money as tips, the guides donate it to the city of Edinburgh.

I find it very heartening in this age of 'take, take, take' to know that there are some people who will perform a service for the sheer pleasure of it and for the honour of helping their city. Certainly the Voluntary Guides of Edinburgh belie all the old Glasgow-versus-Edinburgh jokes about the two cities, which are supposed to be deadly rivals. Glaswegian comics say the best thing about Edinburgh is the Glasgow train leaving Waverley Station. They also joke that whereas in Glasgow a visitor will be asked, 'Will you stay for tea?' the Edinburgh hostess will ask, in a question that permits of only one answer, 'You'll have had your tea?'

When I was performing in the Fringe revue, I wanted to visit the grave of Clarinda, the woman who inspired Robert Burns to write 'Ae Fond

The Mound and Princes Street, looking down on the columns of the National Gallery of Scotland.

Kiss'. But Canongate Church where she is buried is near the foot of the Royal Mile, and I was told that the best way to absorb the atmosphere of old Edinburgh is to start at the top at Edinburgh Castle and then walk all the way down the Royal Mile to the Palace of Holyroodhouse.

Staying with Margaret enabled me to glean in advance many interesting details of the history and buildings of the Royal Mile, but nothing prepared me for the breathtaking view from Edinburgh Castle. To the north, the broad est-·uary of the Forth opens out to the sea, with the

hills of Fife in the background. Nearer at hand are the Salisbury Crags and Arthur's Seat while to the south stretches the magnificent sweep of the Pentland Hills. Westwards, on a clear day, the tops of the Perthshire mountains can be seen, and the whole city lies at your feet like a relief map.

Below the battlements lie Princes Street Gardens, just across the road from the Princes Street shops. I loved to wander round the Gardens looking at the flowers, the fountain and the statues. Among various military ones is the American Memorial to Scots who died in the First World War. This one is very striking, with a background frieze of pipers, drummers and volunteers who answered the call of duty, and in the foreground a young, kilted soldier.

Quite often I would go to the Gardens to listen to the band, or to gaze at the renowned Floral Clock, a first priority for many visitors.

The Floral Clock is an amazing arrangement of 20,000 flowers in the form of a clock. Electrically driven, it is an endless source of fascination to young and old alike to 'watch the flowers move'.

If the Floral Clock is the outstanding feature of the West Princes Street Gardens, the 200-feet-high Scott Monument dominates the gardens to the east. The people of Edinburgh erected this in 1844 to the memory of Sir Walter Scott, and the figure of Scott is imaginatively surrounded with statues of the principal characters from his poems and from the Waverley novels. There is an interior staircase which enables you to climb to the top. The first time I climbed it I counted 286 steps, but since everyone assures me there are 287 I must have missed one somewhere.

You can see the tall pinnacles of the Scott Monument from Edinburgh Castle. The castle is where Edinburgh's history began, if evidence of Iron Age settlements on the castle rocks is to be believed. Edinburgh, like Rome, was built on seven hills, and it was on one of the biggest crags that the earliest settlers constructed their first fortress to withstand enemy attack. In the seventh century, King Edwin of Northumbria made the fortress stronger and some people claim that the name Edinburgh is derived from King Edwin.

The castle has had an exciting history, in which the English have wrested it from the Scots only to have it seized back from them. Indeed, accounts of Edinburgh Castle's past read more like fiction than fact. On one occasion the castle was taken from the English by a group of Scots bearing casks and hampers of gifts. The sentries were so distracted by all the commotion this caused that they were easily captured.

In the fifteenth century, the Duke of Albany managed to escape from his guards by making them drunk and lowering himself down the castle walls. Those castle walls – if only they could talk . . .

Inside the castle there is a great deal to see. It is difficult to know where to begin, but my hostess Margaret had told me that I should not miss the old Royal Palace where the ill-fated Stuarts lived, and where Mary Queen of Scots gave birth to the son who became James VI of Scotland and I of England. In the Crown Room are the gold, pearl-studded crown, sceptre and other insignia of the Honours of Scotland.

In the Crown Square is the Scottish National War Memorial, built in honour of the 100,000 Scots who died in the 1914-18 war, and opposite stands the Great Hall, now the armoury, with its fine timbered roof. A vantage point on the castle rock is St Margaret's Chapel, dedicated to Malcolm Canmore's saintly queen, who did so much to help and reform the Scottish Church. The chapel is so small that only twenty-six people can worship there. The building, which is the oldest in Edinburgh, has an atmosphere that I found very moving, especially when I walked out from there and surveyed the New Town of Edinburgh below me and the ancient kingdom of Fife in the distance.

I always think you should leave a castle by a drawbridge, and that is exactly what you do at Edinburgh. Another thoroughly appropriate tradition there is the one o'clock gun. That year when I was at the Fringe was the first opportunity I had had of having a really good look inside the castle, and I remember that as I was leaving the castle by its drawbridge, the one o'clock gun went off. It so startled me that I nearly fell into the moat underneath. Since then I have gone back to the castle many times as a visitor. But I was there once as an official guest of the government when I was asked to sing for the late Mr Kosygin when he was Prime Minister of the USSR. The concert took place in the Great Hall, and Sir Alexander Gibson (conductor of the Scottish National Orchestra) accompanied me at the piano. The Russians love Scots songs, especially those written by Robert Burns, and Mr Kosygin told me later, when I was presented, how much he had enjoyed listening to them.

I have been back to the castle also as a guest at the Festival Tattoo. It is very difficult to describe such a tattoo to people who have never seen it, for it is far more than a military display. I usually tell them to visualize moonlight, massed pipe bands, dancing and feats of skill and daring by armed forces from the UK and by contingents from abroad. In 1980, for example, as well as our own Queen's Guard, there was a precision drill team from a university in New Brunswick, and the premier bands of Australia and New Zealand. And I will never forget the twenty-four Arab dancing girls who had been sent over by the Sultan of Oman.

Nor shall I forget the two fascinating days during my Fringe engagement that I spent exploring the Royal Mile.

The Royal Mile was once the Old Town of Edinburgh, protected by the castle rock and by the marshland of the Nor' Loch. The protection was admirable, but it meant there was only one way for its citizens to build – upwards. Up, up, up they built to a height of seven to ten storeys, but since space was at a premium, the frontage was narrow and the rooms were small.

What intrigues me about the Royal Mile is that in olden times these high houses were shared by rich and poor alike. A duchess and a dustman might share one of the winding stone staircases. But let me add, hastily, that this was no attempt at class equality. The poor people lived in squalid conditions on the ground floor, and the higher you rose in the house, the more noble was your status. Whilst the ground-floor folk lived in bleak poverty, the top-floor residents lived in rooms with fine furniture and furnishings and painted ceilings. Light streamed in through the top-floor windows and the air was fresher.

There is a story of an eighteenth-century Scottish gentleman who was horrified when he was offered a flat on the ground floor of a London house. He replied angrily that 'he kent very well what gentility was and when he had lived a' his life in a sixth storey he wasna' come to London to live on the grund.'

I cannot say I blame him. There were certainly hazards involved in living on the ground floor on

The Grassmarket and Victoria Street, one of my earliest memories of Edinburgh.

the Royal Mile two hundred years ago, since the residents indulged in the practice of throwing their slops and other refuse out of the window, accompanied by a shout of 'Gardey loo!' *('Gare de l'eau')*. It was hardly hygienic, but in those days there was no underground sanitation.

Within the length of the Royal Mile are several well-known districts: Castlehill, Lawnmarket, High Street and Canongate. If you start your trip near the entrance to the castle at Castlehill, you pass Cannonball House, where a cannonball embedded in one of the gables is supposed to be a relic from the 1745 rising. On the other side of the street is Outlook Tower where the 'camera obscura' — much loved by children — gives a magnified view of the city below you.

'Don't miss Gladstone's Land,' my Royal Mile expert had urged, so I made a point of spending some time there. Gladstone's Land is an old house, dating from the mid-seventeenth century, which has been renovated by the National Trust. Not only has the Trust preserved the outside staircase and the crow-stepped gables of Gladstone's Land, but it has lovingly restored the arcaded ground floor, the painted ceilings and the rooms of the interior to give visitors an instant impression of what life was like in the Old Town.

Gladstone's Land is in the area known as the Lawnmarket, so called because the lawn- or cloth-sellers in the city had their stalls here. In this part of the Royal Mile is Lady Stair's House, built in the eighteenth century. It was presented to the town as a museum and contains some of the manuscripts of Sir Walter Scott, Robert Burns and Robert Louis Stevenson, through which I passed some time browsing.

I liked the idea of Lady Stair's House being in Lady Stair's Close, but then that was the way of old Edinburgh. The occupants of the finest houses often gave their names to the close in which they lived. The infamous Deacon Brodie lived in Brodie's Close. He must have been a strange neighbour for those who lived nearby, for he was a councillor by day and a burglar by night. Robert Louis Stevenson based his character of Dr Jekyll/Mr Hyde on Deacon Brodie. Stevenson was only one of a number of famous men who lived in Edinburgh. Another, the philosopher David Hume, lived in Riddell's Close.

These closes, lanes and wynds are part of the charm of the Royal Mile, as are the circular stair-

ways, cunningly built running anti-clockwise so that defending swordsmen could use their right arms. The intriguing side streets are so inviting that I found it very difficult to keep walking directly downhill, but the beautiful crown steeple of St Giles' Cathedral was my real objective. I could hardly go home at lunchtime to Margaret without having seen St Giles. This Gothic edifice should, strictly speaking, be called the 'High Kirk of St Giles', and there has been a church here since the ninth century.

John Knox, the fiery Calvinist who led the Protestant reformation in Scotland, was minister at St Giles until his death in 1572.

John Knox's grave is in Parliament Square, which is also the location of Parliament House. Here the crimson-robed Scottish judges administer the Scottish legal system, which derives from Roman law and differs from the English system in many respects. When Madeleine Smith was accused of poisoning her lover, the jury found the charge not proven, a verdict unknown to English law. Several plays and films based on the Madeleine Smith case have been made, and I have always considered that the role of Madeleine must be a marvellous challenge for an actress.

When I left Parliament House I found that time had overtaken me, and I had to hurry back to prepare for my evening performance. Margaret was not the least surprised to hear that I had managed to see only half of the Royal Mile, and she strongly advised me to return to it on the following day.

Taking her advice, next morning I explored the southern half of the Royal Mile, which begins at the junction of High Street with North and South Bridge and ends at Holyrood Palace. At the junction is the Tron church, where people come to celebrate Hogmanay. Farther south is John Knox's House. An old building with timbered galleries, it is thought to have been built by the goldsmith to Mary Queen of Scots.

I found the house a little forbidding and was glad to escape into the Museum of Childhood across the street. Now here is a place to delight young and old, crammed with toys, schoolbooks, and all the minutiae of the life of a child of yesteryear, from food to medicines.

In the Canongate Tolbooth can be found another museum, housing a collection of Highland dress and tartans. In this area too there is Huntly

House, one of the most fascinating dwellings in Edinburgh. It has survived from the sixteenth century, and the eighteen rooms in the restored house and its extension contain a unique collection of Edinburgh glass, together with pictures and maps relating to Edinburgh's history. Also on display are personal memorabilia of Earl Haig. The rooms themselves have beautiful panelling and fine fireplaces.

Clarinda's grave, in Canongate churchyard.

I could have spent hours there, but that morning I was determined that I would at last see the grave of Clarinda in the Canongate churchyard.

Clarinda was an Edinburgh woman who was one of the great loves of Robert Burns' life. Unfortunately she was someone else's wife – a Mrs Agnes Maclehose. One November she wrote to Burns to tell him that she was going to join her husband in Jamaica, and before she left Clarinda and Burns had one last meeting in Edinburgh, on 6 December 1791. Burns wrote joyfully:

O May, thy morn was ne'er so sweet
As the mirk night o' December.

But when he returned to Dumfries, the reality of his loss came home to him and he sent this poem to Clarinda.

Ae fond kiss and then we sever
Ae farewell and then forever...

All the poet's misery is expressed in these lines, and the next stanza is even more poignant:

Had we never loved so kindly
Had we never loved so blindly
Never met – or never parted
We had ne'er been broken-hearted.

Mozart was able to express deep emotion in a short phrase and Robert Burns had the same gift. Byron selected this stanza as a motto for his poem 'The Bride of Abydos', and Sir Walter Scott commented that 'one verse [of 'Ae Fond Kiss'] is worth a thousand romances'.

Their praise was by no means too fulsome, in my opinion. To me, 'Ae Fond Kiss' is one of the most beautiful love songs ever written and my only regret is that although it is my favourite song of all I can never sing it. Like 'Annie Laurie', the song is about a man's love for a woman and only a man should sing it.

When you come out of the Canongate churchyard, you can walk down to the Inn and the little houses of White Horse Close, now renovated and restored. Nearer Holyrood, debtors used to find safety in the area known as 'the Sanctuary'.

Then at last you come to the end of the Royal Mile and Holyrood Palace, the official residence of the Queen in Scotland. The architecture of this sixteenth-century palace is French, but its historical associations are closely linked with the Stuarts, especially Mary Queen of Scots. This was where she lived and loved from 1561 to 1567. It was at Holyrood that the Queen's friend, Rizzio, was stabbed by associates of her husband, Darnley, who in turn was later blown up at his house in Kirk o'Field. Many Scots suspected that the Earl of Bothwell was behind Darnley's murder, and there was consternation in Scotland when Mary married him in 1567. Her marriage caused her to lose support in Scotland and flee to England to her cousin Queen Elizabeth, who promptly imprisoned her and ultimately executed her.

When the Queen is not in residence, the Palace is open to the public, who can see the 'Historic Apartments', where the dramatic events in Mary Queen of Scots' life took place, the state apartments and the picture gallery. Our present Queen holds garden parties at Holyrood, too. I have been invited there many times, but must admit that I have rarely gained more than a glimpse of the Queen at these parties. It is when I have been presented to her at Royal Command Performances that I have been close enough to appreciate her startlingly blue eyes and beautiful complexion.

The name Holyrood is derived from the legend that when David I went out hunting on a holy day and was attacked by a stag, he was miraculously saved and left holding a holy cross (or rood) in his hand. He founded the Chapel Royal in the spot where the miracle occurred and it was in this chapel that many of Scotland's kings and queens were buried – including Mary Queen of Scots.

Behind Holyrood Palace is Arthur's Seat, the highest of Edinburgh's seven hills. Since it is only 822 feet, it is an easy climb and a popular spot for picnickers, geologists and artists. One day I would love to paint the view of the mountains, castle and town which you see from the top of Arthur's Seat.

Since my years at the Festival 'Fringe' and my visits to the Military Tattoo, I have taken part in my first pantomime, also in Edinburgh. This was *Babes in the Wood* at the King's Theatre, in which I played Maid Marion. It may sound like a safe role, but it did not materialize as such. My handsome Robin Hood would never have won prizes for archery, and every time one of his arrows went astray I felt certain I had just given my last performance ever!

Just across the waters of the Firth of Forth is the Kingdom of Fife. Fife, the smallest of all the Scottish regions, is unique because it strongly resisted all attempts to put its southern half with Edinburgh into the Lothian region and its northern half into Tayside. Its chief town, Dunfermline, was Scotland's capital for six centuries.

I have always looked forward to visiting friends in Dunfermline, and seeing again the lovely Benedictine Abbey founded by Malcolm Canmore's wife, Queen Margaret. Dunfermline was the birthplace of Andrew Carnegie, who was born in a small cottage in the town and emigrated to America. There he became a multi-millionaire, but he never forgot his home town or his native land, and both have benefited from his vast wealth because he set up trusts which are still administered in Dunfermline.

Another local modern-day philanthropist is the Earl of Elgin, who has used his energy, enthusiasm and resources to raise money for many good causes. Few people realize, in fact, just how much the Earl has achieved and I have been only too happy to help him in a small way.

Another genial Fife friend is Jimmy Shand, the famous band-leader who comes from Auchtermuchty. If ever you want to confound a Sassenach, just ask him to pronounce that word. We Scots just love making the 'ch' as guttural as we can.

Auchtermuchty is a peaceful little village in rich farming country. The bell of Auchtermuchty has featured in some curious stories about the village, which went bankrupt in 1818. Assets were sold, magistrates were jailed and the bell in the parish church (now removed) was found to be one of the silver Lady bells from Lindores Abbey.

Three miles away from there is Falkland, where the simplicity of the weavers' cottages in the village streets contrasts with the magnificence of Falkland Palace, with its fine Flemish tapestries, royal apartments and lovely old walled garden.

Another celebrated spot in Fife is Loch Leven. Mary Queen of Scots was imprisoned on an island in the middle of Loch Leven and made a dramatic escape when young Willy Douglas locked everyone into the great hall when they were at prayers and helped Mary Queen of Scots to a rowing boat he had hidden by the lochside. When he was in the middle of the loch, he dropped the keys to the castle into the water.

The village of Culross, five miles west of Dunfermline, was selected by the Dutch television team for whom I once made a special programme as a background for some of my songs. This Fife village has become something of a showpiece. Many of its buildings have been so cleverly restored by the National Trust that it has retained much of the ambience of a sixteenth-century village, with paved stones, a picturesque old harbour and church and a mercat cross in its small square. The white finish on the external

The distinctive wrought-iron gates of the Palace of Holyroodhouse.

walls of the houses and the bold surrounds on doors and windows are very distinctive.

Culross, and the entire coastline of the East Neuk of Fife, scene of the most picturesque villages in Britain, have also benefited from the Trust's 'little houses' restoration scheme.

After passing through Kinghorn, Kirkcaldy and Buckhaven, you reach Elie, with its fine golf courses and flat, yellow sands.

Then you come to St Monans, one of the fishing villages which the National Trust has transformed. It has bought, renovated and rehabilitated at least twenty of the more unusual houses, and the small cottages which cluster round the harbour are trim and neat. In Pittenweem, Kellie Lodging has a square tower jutting out over the pavement and The Gyles is a three-storey house with an attic in a frontal gable. The mellow old stone, crow-stepped gables and red pantiled roofs of these tall, narrow houses make the harbour uniquely attractive.

In Anstruther, too, the old houses in the narrow streets were renovated under the 'little houses' scheme, as was the group of buildings in Shore Street which local people, with the help of the Trust, made into a sea fisheries museum. Anstruther, or Anster, as it is known locally, has an enthusiastic music society and I went there once, many years ago, to sing in Handel's 'Ode to St Cecilia's Day'.

Further north you come to Crail, where the Trust restored the seventeenth-century Custom House. Ceres is even more unusual because its cottages are grouped round a village green and

every June they hold the Ceres Derby: a horse-race round the green commemorating the men of Ceres who helped Robert the Bruce win the battle of Bannockburn. They returned over the medieval hump-backed bridge, another feature of a village which the historian George Scott Moncrieff called 'the prettiest in Scotland'. In Ceres, the Trust has transformed some cottages and a seventeenth-century Weigh House into the Fife Folk Museum, in which you can see displays relating to almost every aspect of seventeenth-century trades and crafts. I like the carving above the doorway showing a bale being weighed on iron scales with the inscription 'God bless the just!' beside it — a fine incentive for honesty.

One of Fife's local characters was 'The Wee Cooper'.

There was a wee cooper wha' lived in Fife
Nickety nackety noo, noo, noo.
And he hae gotten a gentle wife
Hey willie wallachy, ho John Dougal
Alane co rushety roo, roo, roo.

The wee cooper's wife 'wouldna cook and wouldna spin', but the poem goes on to tell how he eventually cured his wife of her laziness.

Perhaps Fife's main claim to fame is the golfer's mecca, St Andrews. Since Scotland can boast hundreds of golf courses, it is quite something to say that St Andrews outshines them all. But how else can you describe the Royal and Ancient Golf Club, which is the ruling authority on the game throughout the world? The first Scottish trophy was the Silver Club, for which contestants competed at Leith, and you can see a selection of every type of golf club which has ever been used in the R and A's private collection.

Although the R and A is the most prestigious golf club in St Andrews, there are three others which are much used by summer visitors, who flock there not just for the golf and the beautiful sands, but for the charm of a seaside town steeped in history. It has ancient churches, a ruined castle and the oldest university in Scotland. I have cause to remember St Andrews University because the students kidnapped me for one of their Charities Day stunts.

The Forth Road Bridge has made a tremendous difference to Edinburgh because it has made the Kingdom of Fife so accessible, and when I have been singing at concerts in Edinburgh it has been easy enough to carry on to Fife.

My visits to Edinburgh are quite frequent but in one sense you could say that I am there all the time — in the Wax Museum in the High Street. This wax museum, the second biggest in Britain and the third biggest in Europe, rivals Madame Tussaud's and has a 'never-never-land' for children, a chamber of horrors, and over 160 Scottish figures from past to present. 'Moira Anderson' stands there chatting to Andrew Cruickshank while Sean Connery hovers in the background.

At least, that is how it was when I last visited the wax museum — but there is always the fear, whenever I go back there, that I might have been melted down.

The Forth Road Bridge at sunset.

AULD LANG SYNE

Should auld acquaintance be forgot,
And never brought to min'?
Should auld acquaintance be forgot,
And days of lang syne?

It was just after 6 am near Darjeeling. I was looking towards the foothills of the Himalayas, wreathed in cloud and mist, and hoping to catch a glimpse of the second highest mountain in the Himalayas, Katchenjunga, which reveals its shining peak for just a few minutes at that hour of the morning. The clouds lifted momentarily and suddenly in the distance I saw the summit of Katchenjunga. Yet, even as I caught my breath, I could not help thinking of our own mountains in Scotland, which are so near and so visible — not just at dawn but throughout the day and throughout the year. Even if there is mist and rain, at some point in the day you can always catch a glimpse of Scotland's mountains.

I love Scotland for many reasons, but its mountains and hills are at the heart of my affection for it: mountains with streams and trees, hills carpeted with wild flowers, woodland alive with the sound of birdsong.

Kirkintilloch, where I was born, looks towards the Campsie Fells, and when we had a house at Fintry the Campsies were the Himalayas to us children. We played hide-and-seek on the green hillsides in spring and summer, chased rabbits through the heather in the autumn and tobogganed down the snowy slopes in the winter.

On our way to Brora in Sutherland, where we spent so many summer holidays, we passed through some of the most beautiful mountain scenery in Scotland. And in Ayrshire, where I went to school, taught music and set up home after I was married, I always had hills for company. Ayrshire has not only the Carrick hills but views across to the peaks of the Isle of Arran. Many of our Scottish islands are known for their hills, especially Skye, where the wild, awesome beauty of the Cuillins is breathtaking, especially in stormy weather.

I have to admit that the weather in Scotland is sometimes less than ideal. Sometimes gales shriek through the trees, snow makes our roads impassable and it can rain hard enough to make you think a second Flood is imminent. But I like the rain. I like to walk across the golf course and feel the rain on my face and the wind blowing through my hair. Some people say rain is good for your complexion. Whether that is true or not, I cherish memories of walks in wind, rain and snow when there has been a roaring fire to welcome us home.

Curiously enough, rain has been a good omen for me. Many rainy mornings have heralded days which have been happy and memorable. Maybe that is why I was one of the few brides who woke up on her wedding day, looked out of the window and exclaimed, 'Oh good, it's raining!'

Rainy days have had a certain wry humour for me, too. Recently I was photographed at Palacerigg Country Life Park at Cumbernauld near Glasgow by its director, David Stephen, who wanted a shot of me with a day-old fawn. I have never in my life done a photography session on such a wet, stormy day. The fawn obviously did not care much for the weather either, and when David eventually located the creature's hiding-place, the poor wee thing was soaking wet — as I shortly became, too, when it pushed its way into my lap.

Fifty yards or so away, the fawn's father, an enormous royal stag, was pounding up and down looking menacing.

'David,' I said, trying not to sound too apprehensive, 'what about that stag? We're in his field, I've got his fawn and he could charge right at me.'

'Ach, don't worry,' David said nonchalantly. 'See his horns? They've got velvet on them. That means he won't attack.'

I tried — and failed — to feel reassured, and when David announced that he had run out of film and would have to go back up to his house for some more I nearly fainted. All I could see was that big stag coming closer and closer.

'David!' I said firmly. 'What about that stag?'

Walking with Jimmy on a late winter's afternoon. Kirkintilloch can be seen in the distance.

'I told you,' David replied, 'he's in velvet.'

'I don't care if he's in mink. Get me out of here!'

I survived unscathed, though wet, but the memory of that day will always make me smile.

David Stephen is a real Scottish character, but then Scotland is teeming with 'characters' in all walks of life. There are also hundreds of so-called 'ordinary' people who are not ordinary at all because they are blessed with kindliness beyond measure and down-to-earth good humour.

A result of my wettest photographic session ever, and the tiny fawn who was the reason for it.

'Auld Lang Syne' is above all a song about memories — memories of family, friends and home — which, for me, means the Scottish hills. I always wanted to live in a house on a hill and now I have achieved my ambition. The house where I live with my husband is perched on a hill looking down on to the Renfrewshire village of Kilmacolm and across to a range of hills. The third member of our 'family' is Jimmy, the dog you see with me in the boat on Loch Lomond earlier in the book. Jimmy will never win prizes at Cruft's because he is a cross between a collie and a spaniel (we think). I cannot be absolutely sure of his parentage because Stuart and I found

On the golf course which adjoins our garden in Kilmacolm.

Above At home with Stuart in our living room at Kilmacolm.
Left In our steeply-sloping garden, with the house at the top of the hill.

Jimmy one night in Blackpool, where I had been in summer season. He had been run over by a car, and at first we thought he was dead, but since we could not bear to leave that damp bundle at the roadside we took him back to the cottage where I was staying. In the morning we thought we detected a glimmer of life.

The vet who examined him said that he was so badly hurt that he should be put down, but by then Jimmy had looked up at us with his big, brown spaniel's eyes and we could not have had him destroyed for all the world. To cut a long story short, we nursed Jimmy back to health and now he is as devoted to us as we are to him. In the summer of 1980 when I went back to Blackpool for another summer season, Jimmy came too. He sat in my dressing-room when I was on stage and barked loudly if anyone tried to enter without his permission. When we are at home, his tail starts to wag the minute he hears my husband's car in the driveway.

So there we are, Stuart, Jimmy and I, in our 'house on the hill', surrounded by the country-side we know and love so well. Most Scots are very proud and a little emotional about their country, and I am no exception. Sir Walter Scott summed up the feeling in one of his most stirring poems:

Breathes there a man with soul so dead
Who never to himself hath said,
    This is my own, my native land!
Whose heart hath ne'er within him burned
As home his footsteps he hath turned
    From wandering on a foreign strand…

O Caledonia! stern and wild,
Meet nurse for a poetic child!
Land of brown heath and shaggy wood,
Land of the mountain and the flood,
Land of my sires! What mortal hand
Can e'er untie the filial band
That knits me to thy rugged strand!
Still, as I view each well-known scene,
Think what is now and what hath been,
Seems as, to me, of all bereft,
Sole friends thy woods and streams are left;
And thus I love them better still,
Even in extremity of ill.

INDEX